ORTHO Start-to-Fin[ish]

D0472507

Cabinets
& Countertops

Meredith® Books
Des Moines, Iowa

Ortho® Books
An imprint of Meredith® Books

All About Cabinets and Countertops
Editor: Larry Johnston
Contributing Writer: Martin Miller
Senior Associate Design Director: Tom Wegner
Assistant Editor: Harijs Priekulis
Copy Chief: Terri Fredrickson
Copy and Production Editor: Victoria Forlini
Editorial Operations Manager: Karen Schirm
Managers, Book Production: Pam Kvitne,
    Marjorie J. Schenkelberg
Contributing Copy Editor: Steve Hallam
Technical Proofreader: George Granseth
Contributing Proofreaders: Chardel Blaine, Sue Fetters,
    Beth Lastine
Indexer: Barbara L. Klein
Electronic Production Coordinator: Paula Forest
Editorial and Design Assistants: Renee E. McAtee,
    Karen McFadden

Additional Editorial Contributions from Art Rep Services
Director: Chip Nadeau
Designers: lk Design
Illustrator: Dave Brandon

Meredith® Books
Publisher and Editor in Chief: James D. Blume
Design Director: Matt Strelecki
Managing Editor: Gregory H. Kayko
Executive Editor, Gardening and Home Improvement:
    Benjamin W. Allen
Executive Editor, Home Improvement: Larry Erickson

Director, Operations: George A. Susral
Director, Production: Douglas M. Johnston

Vice President and General Manager: Douglas J. Guendel

Meredith Publishing Group
President, Publishing Group: Stephen M. Lacy
Vice President-Publishing Director: Bob Mate

Meredith Corporation
Chairman and Chief Executive Officer: William T. Kerr

Chairman of the Executive Committee: E.T. Meredith III

Photographers
(Photographers credited may retain copyright ©
to the listed photographs.)
L = Left, R = Right, C = Center, B = Bottom, T = Top
Laurie Black: 4TR, 6TL, 23TR,
Laurie Dickson: 8BL, 28CL
Susan Gilmore: 11CR
Jay Graham: 27TR, BR
Bob Greenspan/Bob Greenspan Photography: 7TL
Jamie Hadley: 7TR, 10TR, 26TL
Jim Hedrich/Hedrich-Blessing: 22TL
Hedrich-Blessing Studio: 28BL
Hopkins Associates: 11TL
William Hopkins Sr.: 36 TL (both)
InsideOut Studio: 12, 14, 15, 16, 18, 20, 21, 24, 25, 36, 42,
    43, 88, 89, 90, 91
Jenifer Jordan: 11TR, 29TR
Barbara Elliott Martin: 10TL
Jon Miller/Hedrich-Blessing: 27CR
Mike Moreland: 4BL
Tim Murphy/Foto Imagery: 6TR
Eric Roth: 4TL
Jeffrey A. Rycus/Rycus Associates Photography: 7BR
Gregg Scheidemann/(N)Haus Foto: 21
Dean Tanner/Primary Image: 58
Rick Taylor: 8TL, CL
Wilsonart International: 19

All of us at Ortho® Books are dedicated to providing you
with the information and ideas you need to enhance your
home and garden. We welcome your comments and
suggestions about this book. Write to us at:
    Meredith Corporation
    Ortho Books
    1716 Locust St.
    Des Moines, IA 50309–3023

If you would like to purchase any of our home improvement,
gardening, cooking, crafts, or home decorating and design
books, check wherever quality books are sold. Or visit us at:
meredithbooks.com

If you would like more information on other Ortho
products, call 800-225-2883 or visit us at: www.ortho.com

Note to the Readers: Due to differing conditions, tools,
and individual skills, Meredith Corporation assumes no
responsibility for any damages, injuries suffered, or losses
incurred as a result of following the information published
in this book. Before beginning any project, review the
instructions carefully, and if any doubts or questions remain,
consult local experts or authorities. Because codes and
regulations vary greatly, you always should check with
authorities to ensure that your project complies with all
applicable local codes and regulations. Always read and
observe all of the safety precautions provided by
manufacturers of any tools, equipment, or supplies,
and follow all accepted safety procedures.

CABINET & COUNTERTOP DESIGN **4**

MAKING A MATERIAL DIFFERENCE **12**

PLANNING **30**

DISMANTLING **36**

FACELIFTS **42**

INSTALLING NEW CABINETS **58**

INSTALLING NEW COUNTERTOPS **72**

CARE & MAINTENANCE **88**

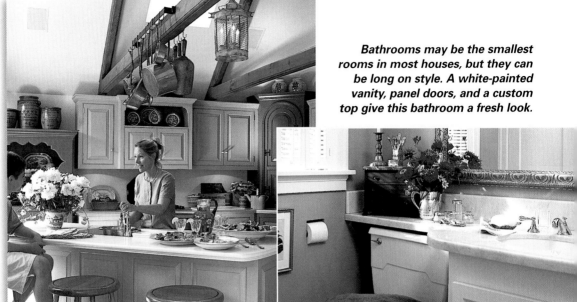

Panel doors create a country or colonial look. Door styles such as these are available from most home centers.

Bathrooms may be the smallest rooms in most houses, but they can be long on style. A white-painted vanity, panel doors, and a custom top give this bathroom a fresh look.

Eurostyle cabinets give a sleek, efficient appearance. You can install flush doors and drawer fronts on existing cabinets to create this look at reasonable a cost.

SURVIVING FACELIFTS AND REMODELING

If cabinet replacement is part of a total kitchen or bathroom renovation, you may not be able to use the room for a week or more. Even putting in new cabinets in an office, children's room, or family room can disrupt the normal family routine. Here are a few tips that can minimize the disruption.

■ No matter where the work area is, keep it cleaned up, especially at the end of each workday. Make arrangements ahead of time for disposal of old cabinets and debris, instead of letting trash pile up.

■ Develop a logical plan for any renovation project. Remove appliances and other permanent fixtures; move them to other locations where you can still use them, if possible.

■ Set up a temporary kitchen (see page 36) and make arrangements with friends or family for showers and bathing.

■ Keep calm and cool. If things get rough and your nerves become frazzled, get away for an evening or a weekend.

CABINET &
COUNTERTOP DESIGN

Cabinets can enhance both the looks and livability of any room. They're usually at center stage in kitchens, but modern design trends are taking cabinetry out of the kitchen and bringing striking, practical arrays into bathrooms, family rooms, dining rooms, and home offices.

Installing your own cabinetry requires only basic carpentry skills and a few hand and power tools—many of which you probably already have in your toolbox or can rent from a local tool rental center. Your cabinet dealer can probably recommend someone to hire for jobs that require special tools or skills.

Completing the job yourself will save you a considerable amount of money—from one-third to one-half of the amount you would pay a professional. In addition, new cabinetry—especially new kitchen installations or units that add organization or convenience to family rooms or home offices—can increase the resale value of your home. The return on your time and labor goes beyond money; when you finish the job, you can take pride in your accomplishment.

In this book, you will find everything from design tips to techniques for dismantling your existing units and installing new ones. If you don't want or don't need to replace the existing cabinets, refinishing or refacing may be the option you're looking for. This book includes step-by-step instructions for these solutions too. And if you choose to contract all or part of the work, the knowledge of materials and construction techniques you'll learn from this book will give you the confidence you need in overseeing or reviewing the work of the professionals you hire.

FINDING THE STYLE THAT'S RIGHT FOR YOU

When choosing a new cabinet style or selecting cabinets for a renovation project, follow these hints to make the decision easier:

■ To start, buy some home decorating magazines from your home center and check out books on kitchen design from your library. When you find a photograph of a cabinet installation that appeals to you, cut it out or make a copy of it. Put the clippings and copies in a manila folder.

■ Visit kitchen showrooms and tour designer homes, making notes about things you like and don't like. Keep these notes in the folder too.

■ When you visit friends' homes, ask about their cabinets. Find out what materials they like and why, and ask about maintenance requirements.

■ Get material samples and color chips from cabinet dealers and home centers. Put them where you will install your new cabinets and look at them in different kinds of light and at different times of day.

■ When you're ready to make decisions, take everything out of the folder and spread it on a table. Discard unappealing designs or those that obviously won't fit within your budget. Settle on those that you like, that you can afford, and that match your do-it-yourself skills. Then pick the best of those.

A GALLERY OF STYLE

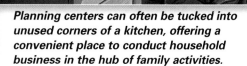

Planning centers can often be tucked into unused corners of a kitchen, offering a convenient place to conduct household business in the hub of family activities.

Islands increase work space in a kitchen and can add eating space. Make sure you have enough room on all sides before installing an island.

Style and design may seem like abstract qualities, but bringing a certain style into a room—or fitting new cabinets into an existing layout—is really an uncomplicated process. Success depends on balance—combining elements that are aesthetically pleasing to you in a way that enhances the comfort and practicality of a given room. Practicality is critical; functional design demands it.

DESIGN FOR USE

Before you start shopping for cabinets and countertop materials, take an inventory of your existing cabinets or survey the room where you will set the new units. Then make a list of all the uses you can imagine—both for the room and for the cabinetry.

FAMILY LIVING SPACE: If you want an entertainment center in the family room or entertaining area, make sure you include space for CDs, DVDs, VHS tapes, and even those impossible-to-part-with vinyl records. Surround your fireplace with base cabinets and bookcases to make the fireplace the focal point of the room. Try combining wine racks with a contemporary wet bar.

HOME OFFICES: Office installations should include comfortable work surfaces, drawer units for files, and shelves that provide both space for decorative items and easy access to current projects.

KITCHENS: New kitchen cabinets offer a wonderful opportunity to add storage and increase efficiency while changing the look of the room. If you reface or paint your existing cabinets, you can rearrange the layout for increased convenience. A couple of base cabinets or island cabinets add storage and dining space that make your daily routine more enjoyable. You can create a more practical layout and change the look of the kitchen by installing unfinished units. Topping off a base cabinet with open shelves and molding can make it look like a freestanding hutch.

Once you complete the list of uses for the room, make it into a checklist. Then as you shop, you can keep track of the features each cabinet line offers and record design details that you think are important.

MAKING SMALL KITCHENS LOOK LARGER

Small kitchens can be challenging, but by thinking simply, you can make them appear more spacious.

■ Keep your design style uncomplicated. A Eurostyle look, with bright laminated surfaces, simple pulls, and invisible hinges, won't look as busy and will seem to take up less room than darkly finished wood with raised-panel doors.

■ Keep color schemes neutral and limit the number of color changes. A dark red tile on a backsplash might look like a stunning border to your dark blue countertop, but will tend to make a small room feel closed in. The cabinets don't necessarily have to be the same color as everything else in the kitchen; just use colors that are tints, shades, or tones of each other.

■ Minimize clutter. Include storage units in your design—tilt trays at the sink, appliance garages for countertop appliances, and plenty of places to hide large utensils and pans.

DESIGN TRENDS

Design often reflects regional tastes, so different styles are more common in different parts of the country. The traditional look is a favorite in some areas; in others,

The massive legs and the apron on this vanity make it look like a piece of furniture rather than built-in cabinetry.

Simplicity and neutral colors make a small kitchen seem larger.

contemporary styles are the standard. The details and definition of style categories change over time too.

TRADITIONAL styles typically feature wood—usually oak, maple, or cherry—with raised-panel doors. Some traditional styles are capped with a large crown molding. Dark finishes were once favorites, but lighter finishes are more in style now. Glazing—a clear or colored top coat applied to stained wood—brings subtle two-toned coloring to cabinets and can suggest a country decor. Glazes also highlight the architecture of the raised door panels.

FRENCH COUNTRY OR RESTORATION is derived from traditional styles and often features rubbed-on glazes that make the cabinets look like they were painted ages

ago and have dust in the corners. These elements are often combined with features that make cabinets look like furniture—legs, feet, and detailed moldings and carvings.

CONTEMPORARY is a broadly applied term. It could apply to anything from laminate-covered surfaces with recessed wooden pulls to the simple, uncomplicated lines of frame-and-flat-panel doors. Contemporary moldings are almost always smaller and more understated than traditional-style moldings. Unlike the sleek, hard-edged, almost industrial appearance of contemporary styles during their debut about 50 years ago, modern contemporary is softer. Even high-tech versions of this style frequently offset the clinical look of stainless-steel cabinets or countertops with a sprinkling of wood and warmer accents throughout.

HARDWARE—pulls, knobs, and hinges—ranges from traditional brass knobs to chrome and brushed metal tubular accents that enhance a contemporary design. The choice of hardware can define the character of standard cabinetry and enhance the design of any installation.

QUICK FIX: REPAIR SCRATCHES

Scratches and dents detract from the appearance of your cabinets, but a few simple repairs can help make them look nice again.

■ Scratch-repair formulas for wood are available at hardware stores or home centers. They come in different colors so you can match the color of your wood. Buy a couple you think match closely; if one or the other doesn't work, mixing them may work.

■ Scratched or damaged laminate can be repaired. Removing a laminate piece is not easy but it's less expensive than a complete cabinet makeover. See page 88 for tips on hiding scratches.

When you lay out your kitchen cabinets, create workstations—spots near the sink, stove, oven, and serving areas that make room for cooking.

A Gallery of Style
continued

Laminate facing is a durable, easy-to-clean cabinet surface that comes in a variety of colors and patterns. Laminate refacing is an affordable way to upgrade existing cabinets.

Custom-built cabinetry is the ultimate kitchen upgrade. Hiring a kitchen designer and a custom builder will be costly, but you will get exactly the look and function you want from your new kitchen.

A ceramic tile countertop may be all you need to brighten up a kitchen or bath. You'll probably need to build a new base for the tile countertop and backsplash, but you can easily complete the job in a couple of weekends.

RENOVATION OPTIONS

When it's time to revitalize the appearance of your kitchen (or any other) cabinetry, you have several options.

PAINTING OR REFINISHING: Changing the finish on existing cabinets is the least expensive option. Just painting dark wood cabinets white or some bright color makes an amazing change. You can add new hardware to define the style as either contemporary or traditional. See pages 44–48.

REPLACING DOORS AND DRAWER FRONTS: Replacing doors is a moderately priced alternative to replacing cabinets. If your wooden cabinets are in good condition, replacing slab doors with raised-panel doors—or vice versa—will make everything look new. Laminate-covered doors in a light wood color work well on wood cases stained a light color. If you have surface-mounted hinges, it's best to reuse the old hardware or install new hardware that has fasteners spaced exactly the same as the old ones. See page 56–57.

REPLACING DOORS AND REFACING THE CABINETS: Changing the outer surface of the cabinets with wood veneer or plastic laminate gives about the same effect as buying new cabinets—at a fraction of the cost. If you like your present layout, but just don't like the way it looks, refacing is the way to go. See pages 50–55.

REPLACING CABINETS WITH NEW ONES: If you want to change both the look and the layout, then new cabinets are the

QUICK FIX:
SPLURGE ON DETAILS

Adding details to existing cabinets and giving them a thorough cleaning can make them look brand-new.

■ Install a colorful tile backsplash along the back of a countertop that doesn't have one. Accent tiles can become the focal point of the kitchen.

■ Change the hardware. Purchase custom knobs or pulls in a different style or finish for a new look at reasonable cost.

■ Add crown molding to cabinets with raised-panel doors to enhance an already traditional look.

■ Put glass-pane doors on some wall cabinets. In many cases, you can rout out the solid door panel and put in glass.

answer. Installing new cabinets can also be the least time-consuming of all your options. See pages 62–67.

BUILDING YOUR OWN CABINETRY: You could save half the cost or more of installing new factory-made cabinets this way, but it requires time, woodworking skills, and a well-equipped workshop. See pages 68–71.

KITCHEN PLANNING

If your plans call for complete remodeling, build efficiency and convenience into the design. Even if you're only refinishing the cabinets, consider simple changes that might make cooking and dining easier.

Theories of kitchen planning have changed over the years. The *work triangle* concept, dating from the 1950s, arranged food preparation, cooking, and storage areas within a triangle. The total perimeter of the triangle (the combined length of its sides) was ideally between 15 feet and 22 feet.

The work triangle reflected household norms of the day: a one-cook kitchen (most women stayed at home and prepared meals with fresh ingredients) with storage for about 400 items.

Current design theories base the kitchen arrangement on *work centers.* The work-center idea reflects different household norms: a kitchen that can accommodate more than one cook (many couples both work outside the home, share cooking activities, and prepare packaged foods more often than in the 1950s) with storage for about 800 items.

The schemes are not mutually exclusive, so both may apply to your kitchen layout. If two people in your family often cook together, for instance, you may want two preparation areas and perhaps a second sink. Separate them to avoid cramping anyone's movement. You may want to add a snack station too, for quick-fix meals for large or active families.

Identify your work-space needs, then fit them into the kitchen, following the work triangle dimensions wherever possible. Each work center needs at least 6 square feet—36 inches of length on a standard (24 inches deep) countertop.

Workstations may reduce the amount of available storage space. To make up for the loss, consider a pantry with swing-out doors and shelves.

Here are some other ideas to consider as you plan your kitchen.
■ A conventional oven is likely to be the least-used major appliance in your kitchen. You can safely locate it (and its work center) outside the main area.
■ In a household with two cooks, create more workstations or larger ones. And you'll

QUICK FIX: REPAIR DAMAGE

Repairing damaged surfaces can freshen your existing cabinets. Remove sagging doors; fill fastener holes with glue and tightly fitting wood slivers (sometimes a kitchen match is just the right size). Then rehang the doors when the glue dries. For doors with open joints, remove and force the joint open gently. Inject carpenter's glue with a squeeze bottle equipped with a thin metal tip (available at your hardware store) and clamp the joint for at least an hour.

Laminate repair kits are available in a wide variety of colors. Repaired laminate may not look like new, but its appearance will be less distracting than the damaged surface.

probably need two sinks. The second sink doesn't need to be as large as the primary one, but should be larger than a small bar sink.
■ Pantries are more convenient when close to food preparation areas. Pantry doors should open away from the workstation for maximum convenience.

WORKSTATIONS VS. WORK TRIANGLES

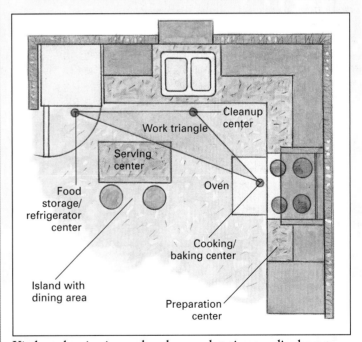

Kitchen planning is now based on workstations; earlier layouts were based on a work triangle. (See text at left.) The two layout theories are not incompatible, however. Notice how the new island in this kitchen provides easy access from the serving area to the dining center. The new wall-mounted oven is slightly outside the existing cooking center. None of the added or rearranged work centers has substantially changed the original work triangle layout.

A GALLERY OF STYLE

continued

Glass panes in cabinet doors add sparkle and make the cabinet contents part of the kitchen decor.

Paint, new hardware, and new doors with glass panes give the existing cabinets in this kitchen a new look at moderate cost. A new tile countertop and backsplash set off the rejuvenated cabinetry.

■ Standard height for countertops is usually 36 inches, but some workstations may be more convenient if the top is 2 to 4 inches lower. Counters 38 inches high are handy for tall people.

■ Include in-kitchen dining if you have the space. Islands or unused corner nooks that are out of the way of food preparation tasks are ideal places to add dining space without interfering with kitchen traffic flow.

■ Add an office. Commonly called a planning center when added to a kitchen, the spot should include computer space, work surface, and some undercounter storage. Place it as far as possible from the sink and stove or other wet or greasy areas.

HOME OFFICE DESIGN

Technology, computers, and the Internet have radically changed lifestyles. Increasing numbers of people are working out of their homes, shopping online, or just adding some office space where they can take care of routine household business.

Because home offices are relatively new to home design, you may have to convert existing space—a spare bedroom or a corner of the kitchen—in an older home. Wherever you put the office, organization is critical. Here are some questions to answer as you plan your office space.

■ Do I need one work center or two?

■ How do I want to position the computer keyboard and the line of sight to the monitor? Keyboard pullouts are one solution; desktop locations are another. Will putting it on the desktop leave enough work space?

If you can, sit in the proposed office location and imagine its arrangement to make sure that key items are within arm's reach.

■ How much file space do I need? Should files be standard letter size, legal, or both?

■ Do I need locking units?

When you have the answers, make a rough sketch showing the cabinet layout and desk space. Take it with you when you shop; add style details as you learn what the market has to offer. You can choose features compatible with the overall room design.

DESIGN PROS

Working with interior designers can make planning a cabinet layout much easier. Even if the only feature of the room you're changing is its cabinetry, a trained designer can often see possibilities that will look dazzling without costing too much. Paying for design services in advance often saves you money by helping you make practical decisions early in the process.

You can find designers in the Yellow Pages, but it's better to start with the recommendations of friends or cabinet dealers. Some retailers have a designer on staff or contract with outside designers. Don't overlook model homes and design open houses. If you see a design you like, make a note of the design firm, if credited, or contact the home builder for information.

Striated green paint on the existing cabinets and a new clay-color countertop brighten this kitchen.

ENTERTAINMENT CENTERS

Television and home-audio technology have brought home a new use for cabinetry: the entertainment center. Most people don't go out for entertainment as often as in decades past; entertainment technology brings it to the home. Installing cabinetry to contain the equipment and make it fit into the home's decor is becoming more popular.

Consider these questions when planning.
■ How much space will be needed to house the television and sound system? Large-screen television sets require relatively deep enclosures. LCD and other digital displays can be wall mounted. A basic stereo system won't require as much space as a system with a large surround-sound receiver, several source devices, and a speaker for the center channel.
■ Will the TV be enclosed to its edges, leaving only the screen visible?
■ Will doors conceal the TV screen or other components of the system when not in use?
■ Will the unit be devoted to entertainment only or will it be surrounded by shelving for curios or books? Will the shelves be open or have doors with (or without) glass?
■ Will the unit be built in or designed as a freestanding piece of furniture?
■ How much space will tapes, discs, and other media and accessories require?

BATH DESIGN

Designing cabinets for a bathroom is easier than for any other room because bathrooms are usually the smallest rooms in the house. Although size may limit your options, plan bathroom cabinet layouts with the same care as you would any other room. For example, make sure there will be enough room to open the vanity's doors and drawers without interference and that the storage area is large enough for your needs. You won't have much

Painting (above) and clear finishing (left) give cabinets of similar style different looks.

control over size if you order a stock vanity; most models are available in only a few standard widths.

Don't overlook the medicine cabinet. It can contribute as much to convenience and style as any other element. You have almost as many options with medicine cabinet doors as with other cabinets.

Doors can either swing on hinges or slide. Some cabinets will solve space problems by mounting in a corner. Three-panel mirrors create a view of almost 180 degrees. Choose the frame material that matches the construction of the vanity, and be sure the cabinet size is proportional to the vanity. If it's too big, it will overwhelm the vanity and the room. If it's too small, the room will feel off balance.

Familiarize yourself with material choices before making your final decision. Keep a scrapbook or folder of design ideas, tour designer homes, and visit your local home centers to help you plan.

MATERIAL SELECTION MADE EASY

A little organization will help you select materials easily from the many choices.

■ Familiarize yourself with available options before you start shopping. Form preliminary opinions about what appeals to you so you can eliminate some of the choices early on.

■ Make style decisions first, then address questions about quality, maintenance, durability, and other functional issues.

■ Ask a lot of questions. Don't make a decision on any material until you feel you have all the answers you need.

■ When choosing cabinets, concentrate on doors. More than any other component, doors define the style for the rest of the installation. Pick the material first, then the color, then the architectural style. Make sure the cabinets are well-built too.

MAKING A MATERIAL DIFFERENCE

Manufactured cabinets come in many materials, styles, and finishes. Custom-built cabinets can be made from almost any available material. And countertops can be made of almost anything, from plastics to stone. Each material, of course, imparts its own design characteristics to a room, and each has advantages and drawbacks.

Plastic laminate, for example, is inexpensive compared to some other countertop materials. In your kitchen, its low price, attractive range of colors and patterns, and ease of cleanup may outweigh its low scratch-resistance to make it the most attractive choice. Granite will stand up to almost anything and is hard to beat for sheer elegance. But granite stains and is costly to install, so you may decide these factors outweigh its beauty.

Allow plenty of time when you research cabinet and countertop materials. Once you install them, you can't easily or inexpensively change your mind. Careful selection will ensure that the cabinets you put in today will retain their appeal for many years.

Pay special attention to the sections of this chapter that apply to the changes you plan to make. If you haven't made up your mind about what renovation method you will use, read the entire chapter before going shopping for cabinets and countertops. The information will give you a thorough look at modern cabinet and countertop materials and construction methods—and how you can apply them to any room in the house.

PLANNING QUESTIONNAIRE

These questions will help you decide how to match cabinet and countertop materials to design styles. You may not know the answers until you finish your shopping. And you may want to reconsider some of your answers to the questions as you learn more.

■ What is the predominant style in the room and in the rest of the house —contemporary, traditional, Southwestern, high-tech?

■ Do you want the installation to match the current decor or to function as an attractive accent on its own?

■ What color combination would best achieve that goal?

■ Considering appearance only, what material appeals to you (wood, plastic laminate, other)?

■ How do installation requirements affect your choice of materials?

■ Do maintenance requirements for a material or limitations in its use make you feel more or less positive about it? Will it meet the demands of your lifestyle? If not, consider an alternative—using cutting boards, for example, on laminate surfaces.

CHOOSING DOOR STYLES

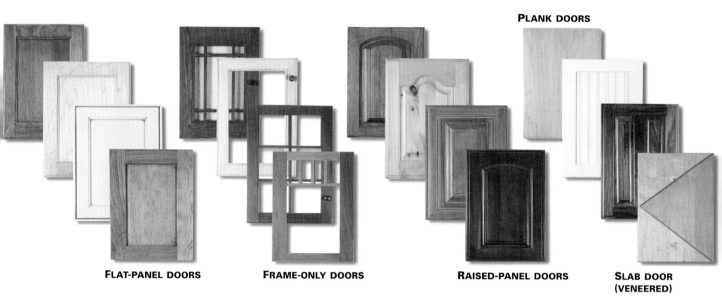

PLANK DOORS

FLAT-PANEL DOORS　　**FRAME-ONLY DOORS**　　**RAISED-PANEL DOORS**　　**SLAB DOOR (VENEERED)**

Doors define the style of cabinets. Some of their distinguishing features are their shape, their construction, and the kind of hardware installed.

To some extent, all of these elements vary with the type of door material—wood, plastic laminate, rigid thermal foil (RTF), or other synthetics.

DOOR OVERLAYS

The way doors fit the cabinet face affects their appearance as much as paneling or accents.

Inset doors fit inside the face frame opening, flush with its front surface.

Lipped doors have rabbeted back edges, forming a lip that rests on the front of the face frame.

Overlay doors are mounted on the front of the frame, and depending on whether they are partial or full, conceal all or part of the face frame.

WOOD

Wood doors are assembled in different ways, depending on their style.

SLAB DOORS are flat pieces of plywood or medium-density fiberboard (MDF) covered on both sides with wood veneers, often with a higher grade on one side. Of the two substrates, MDF is the least likely to warp. Slab doors are suited primarily to a full overlay style. (See "Door Overlays," at left.)

PLANK DOORS are flat doors made from solid softwood or hardwood boards. They have more design potential than slab doors because the grain pattern changes from board to board. Decorative patterns may be cut into the door face. Plank doors are more likely to warp, but battens fastened to the back of the door can minimize warping.

FRAME-AND-PANEL DOORS are manufactured with a four-piece frame that surrounds a central panel. The panel may be flat or raised. Panels can be configured in a number of ways—various types of arched-top panels or rectangular styles are most common.

FRAME-ONLY DOORS are rabbeted on the inside back edge to accept a glass pane. The frame may be wide or narrow, and muntins are often installed to divide the glass into sections, known as lights.

PLASTIC LAMINATE

Plastic-laminate doors are similar to slab doors in appearance. Most of them have a ⅝-inch MDF core covered with plastic laminate on the front, back, and edges. (The edges are usually covered with PVC to avoid the laminate edge line.) This style is almost always used for overlay doors. You'll find hundreds of colors and patterns, including wood grains. Some have embossed textures, which are more difficult to keep clean.

RIGID THERMAL FOIL

An RTF door is a ¾-inch MDF slab with a sheet of heat-formed PVC on its face. These doors come in slab styles or with a raised-panel design routed into the core before the plastic coating is applied. The RTF surface is not as tough as plastic laminate and won't stand up to cleaning with mild abrasives. Although they can resemble their plastic-laminate relatives, RTF door designs are more limited, and the process of manufacture does not produce details that are as crisp. Corners and edges are somewhat rounded. Other synthetic coverings, such as polyester, are applied in a similar manner and have similar wear properties.

CHOOSING A STYLE

With so many materials and styles available, picking a door style that suits your tastes may seem mind-boggling. Whether you are refacing your cabinets or installing new ones, you can reach a decision more easily by breaking the process down into three steps.
CHOOSE THE MATERIAL YOU LIKE: This choice will be affected not only by appearance and maintenance requirements, but by budget. Wood will almost always be more expensive, followed by plastic laminate

DRAWER FRONTS

The style of your drawer fronts should generally match the style of your doors—slab fronts look better with slab doors, raised panels with raised-panel doors.

When selecting a raised-panel style, purchase the thickest material you can afford. Drawer fronts made from ⁵⁄₄ stock look more substantial than thinner ones, and the extra thickness will give your hinge screws more wood to bite into.

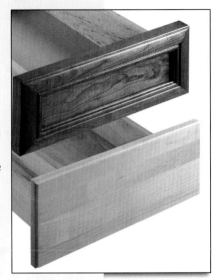

and other synthetic coverings. Wood will usually lend itself to applications in more rooms than the other materials, adding warmth and character to living rooms, dining rooms, family environments, and offices.
CHOOSE A COLOR: Take into account the rest of the design elements in the room and the aspects of overall style. If you're remodeling an entire room, you can make your cabinets a focal point. If you're changing only the cabinetry, you can make it harmonize with the existing color scheme.
DECIDE ON DESIGN: Select flat- or raised-panel doors. If you want raised panels, decide between cathedral and rectangular panels. Stained, painted, or distressed, flat doors enhance a country style. Covered with plastic laminate, the same doors can create a contemporary European look. Raised panels have the look of tradition and elegance.

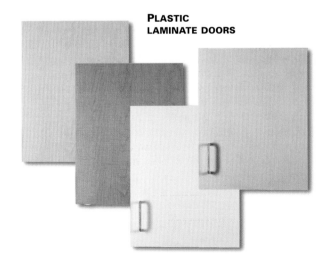

PLASTIC LAMINATE DOORS

RIGID THERMAL FOIL DOORS

THE WOOD LOOK

Oak | Maple | Cherry | Hickory | Pine

Oak
Cherry
Pine
Hickory
Maple

Grain patterns and coloration vary widely among wood species. Choose the grain pattern first, then color. The samples above show the natural color of each wood with a clear finish and no stain. The photos at top right show the woods with different stains.

Wood holds a prominent place in cabinet construction. To some, no other material can equal the richness and elegance of real wood. Properly finished with polyurethane or catalyzed finishes, wood will stand up to all but the hardest use. And with quality materials and design, you won't have to change your cabinet style for a long time.

Whether you buy prefinished cabinets or purchase or build unfinished units, choosing the right wood comes down to the same criteria as any other design decision—you have to balance aesthetics with practicality. This means choosing among species of wood.

WOOD SPECIES

Nature makes wood in many species, which fall into two categories that have somewhat

SOLID WOOD OR LAMINATE?

Although some homeowners have a definite preference for wood cabinetry, wood does have some drawbacks. You can't scrub off dried food spills readily without damaging the finish. And even though modern finishes are tough and durable, wood dents, scratches, and can chip or crack with severe abuse.

Plastic laminate comes in a wide range of colors and even embossed patterns. It may not have the rich appearance of wood, but it will be consistent in color, easy to clean up, and more resistant to abuse. In formal settings, such as dining rooms, plastic laminate may have a more limited design potential.

misleading names—hardwoods and softwoods. (See the chart opposite.) The distinction between them is based on botany: Hardwood comes from trees that lose and regrow their leaves with changes of season, softwood comes from coniferous trees. And while many softwoods are indeed softer than hardwoods, some are not. Here's a brief survey of woods commonly found in cabinetry, starting with some popular hardwoods.

OAK: In two species—red and white—this hardwood is a traditional favorite. Red oak is a red-orange color, which looks rich even under clear finishes. White oak is more neutral. Both species are hard and display a wide variety of grain patterns, but their surfaces—even when filled and sanded—feel somewhat uneven to the touch. This is characteristic to the species and can help hide minor dings and dents.

MAPLE: In some parts of the country, the harder variety of this close-grained species has become more popular than oak. In its natural state, it is the whitest of woods, but because it has a grain pattern similar to cherry, it can give the look of that more expensive species if finished with a cherry stain. Be careful when choosing maple—don't select cabinets with doors or frames that have knots and streaks.

CHERRY: Somewhat more expensive than either oak or maple, cherry is a close-grained, sometimes highly figured hardwood that is dense, hard, and durable. Cherry mellows with age into a warm, rich patina that shows best with a light stain or clear finish.

OTHER HARDWOODS: Birch, poplar, and aspen are used in unfinished cabinetry. They take paint well. Teak, mahogany, walnut, and

WOOD SPECIES: A QUICK COMPARISON

	Grain/color	Stability	Cost	Comments
SOFTWOODS				
Pine, Fir, Whitewoods	Little figure/light	Moderate	Low	Used for painted surfaces
HARDWOODS				
Oak	Figured/medium	High	Moderate	Red oak used widely in cabinets
Maple, Birch	Little figure/light	High	Moderate	Birch is often used for painted work
Cherry, Pecan, Hickory	Highly figured/ light	High	Moderate/ high	Best for fine cabinetry

custom cabinetry, but are rarely seen in manufactured cabinets. Exotic hardwoods could be incorporated to create cabinetry that rivals fine furniture. Some species are difficult to work and all are expensive. Check with your woodworking supplier if you want to build or have cabinets built from these woods. **SOFTWOODS:** Most softwoods dent more easily than any of the hardwoods, but are well suited to country kitchen settings or for painted and distressed designs. Pine and fir are the most common softwoods for cabinetry.

COLOR AND FINISH

The color of your wood cabinets depends on the type of finish you use. A clear finish will show the wood grain; the color will vary slightly depending on the finish. Clear finishes will not, however, hide imperfections, glue lines, or joints. In fact, clear finishes may accentuate them.

Dark pigmented stains can obscure the grain and will change the color of any wood species. Medium stains often bring out the best color and grain qualities of the wood. Dye stains show the grain better than pigmented stains. Stains are available in a range of wood tones and colors suited for most decorating schemes.

Finishes also affect the durability of cabinets. In kitchens and baths, apply a high-gloss oil-base paint or polyurethane varnish for long wear and easy cleanup. Rubbed-on oil finish or satin lacquer provides a softer look that might be more appropriate for an office or formal dining room where durability is not so important.

CHOOSING THE RIGHT FINISH

If you plan to purchase unfinished cabinets and doors, or to build your own units, pay special attention to the type of finish you apply. Here is a brief look at some of your options.

	Application	Resistance to Stains/Abrasion/Fading	Repairs	Comments
Oil-base paint (high-gloss enamels)	Brush	High/Moderate/High	Recoat	Requires priming and two finish coats
Latex-base paint	Brush/roller	Moderate/Moderate/Moderate	Recoat	Inexpensive varieties not durable
Milk paint (casein)	Brush	High/High/High	Recoat	Gives antique look under varnish
Oil/varnish	Brush/rags	Moderate/Moderate/High	Recoat	Some products offer quick drying times
Gelled varnish	Rags	Moderate/High/High	Recoat	Much easier application than brush-on varnishes
Oil-base polyurethane	Brush/spray	Moderate/High/High	Strip, sand, recoat	A hard finish, very difficult to remove
Water-base urethane	Brush	Moderate/High/High	Strip, sand, recoat	A hard finish, very difficult to remove
Oils	Brush/rag	Low/Low/Moderate	Recoat	Generally not durable enough for kitchen and baths, but excellent for fine cabinetry
Lacquer	Brush/spray	High/High/High	Recoat	Excellent for fine cabinetry not subject to hard use

REFACING MATERIALS

Refacing your existing cabinets is a cost-effective means of changing the look of your room. Only painting or refinishing costs less. Some local home centers stock refacing materials, including doors and drawer fronts, but you will probably find a larger selection of higher-quality materials at refacing suppliers, many of whom do business on the Internet.

CHOOSING DOORS FOR REFACING

Slab doors are the only style suitable for direct application of veneer or laminate. If you have any other style, you'll have to order replacement doors and drawer fronts.

Choose replacement doors by following the same general method you would if you were purchasing new cabinets. Choose the material

REFACE OR REPLACE?

Refacing cabinets costs less than buying new ones, even if you install the new cabinets yourself. But cost is not the only consideration. Some cabinets—metal ones, for example—can't be easily refaced. Metal cabinets are usually removed and replaced with new cabinets.

If you like the layout and configuration of your existing cabinets, if they are square, level, and in good repair with only minor surface damage, and if you have the skills and time to do the job, then refacing makes sense. If you need additional cabinet space, you can build or buy unfinished cabinets, install them, and reface them at the same time.

first, then the color, then the design. Wood doors will usually require wood veneer on cabinet surfaces, and synthetic doors will work best with plastic laminate cabinet faces.

Wood doors are available prefinished or unfinished. Whatever style you choose, buy all the materials from the same manufacturer so the elements are compatible. If you decide to use unfinished doors, make sure you can finish them with products that have the same appearance as your finished veneer. Water-base urethanes are tough, and their application does not require specialized skills or equipment.

WOOD VENEER

Wood veneer is real wood, sliced from logs in thin layers (about $\frac{1}{40}$ inch thick). Veneer adhered to a paper backing is available in both unglued and preglued sheets. Sheet sizes are commonly 2×8 feet, but some manufacturers make 4×8-foot sheets. The larger size might result in less waste but can also prove difficult to handle in small work areas. You can easily reface most cabinet surfaces using the smaller sheets.

Veneer itself is rather fragile, but properly adhered, it is as strong and durable as its substrate (in this case, your existing cabinets). And if severe damage requires replacement of a piece, it's difficult but not impossible to remove. Preglued veneer is slightly more expensive, but its convenience is worth the added expense.

Application starts with cutting the sheets slightly oversize, aligning them, and adhering. Unglued sheets require application of contact adhesive—either sprayed or brushed on—to both the cabinet and veneer. Preglued products may have a hot-glue backing that softens as you apply it with a household iron. Or they may have pressure-sensitive adhesive protected by a removable paper backing. Even though pressure-sensitive veneer is self-sticking, application of contact adhesive to the frame will produce a stronger bond.

COVERING THE SIDES

The end stiles (the vertical members) slightly overhang the sides on most cabinets, some by as much as $\frac{1}{4}$ inch. The thin sheets of veneer will not make up the difference, so you must make the surfaces flush. You can either trim the stile with a plane or router, or build up the side with plywood or other material.

■ **PLYWOOD:** The least expensive way to cover cabinet sides is with $\frac{1}{8}$-inch- or $\frac{1}{4}$-inch-thick plywood with one good hardwood face. The thinner stock cuts more easily, but you may find it doesn't lie as flat. Whatever thickness you apply, choose a hardwood and a grain pattern that matches your veneer. Pre-finish the plywood to match the color and final finish of the cabinets. Fasten it to the sides of the unit with construction adhesive and brads (see page 70). Local home centers may carry plywood of sufficient quality for refacing. If yours does not, order it from a refacing specialty outlet.

PHENOLIC VENEER: This wood veneer bonded to a 4×8-foot sheet of plastic laminate is stiffer than plywood and somewhat more difficult to cut and work with. It easily hides surface imperfections in the cabinet sides. Apply it with contact adhesive. Its 1/16-inch thickness makes it too stiff to wrap around the edges of cabinet frames.

THREE-PLY VENEER: This material has three layers of wood and no paper backing. It cuts more easily than other materials and installs with contact adhesive.

PLASTIC LAMINATES

Plastic laminates are made from layers of kraft paper impregnated with plastic resins and bonded together with heat and high pressure (see page 26). The result is a sheet about 1/16 inch thick that is hard, stain-resistant, and easy to clean, but is brittle and easy to chip. Laminate comes in a wide variety of colors and textures. Solid-color laminates, which are slightly more expensive, do not reveal a brown edge when trimmed.

Available in a large number of solid colors and patterns, plastic laminate is a popular and versatile choice for both countertops and cabinet facing.

Laminate comes in three thicknesses—vertical grade (.035 inch) for doors and sides, post-forming grade (.040 inch) for heat-forming, and horizontal grade (.050 inch) for countertops. It is adhered with contact adhesive, following one of two methods. (See "Plastic Laminate Installation" below.)

Vinyl laminates are available to match RTF doors, but vinyl won't bend around corners on the frames. As an alternative, cover the edges with plastic laminate of a closely matching color or paint the edges of the frames before applying the vinyl.

PEEL-AND-STICK OR IRON-ON?

Before you purchase either kind of veneer, consider the pros and cons. Prefinished pressure-sensitive veneers—peel-and-stick—are somewhat more difficult to align and install than the iron-on variety. Pulling back the paper backing and applying the veneer straight at the same time may seem unwieldy at first. Practice with scrap material until you get the hang of it.

Iron-on veneers are much easier to align. However, they may end up taking more time to install than the peel-and-stick products. Iron-on veneers are usually unfinished, so you will need to finish your cabinets after refacing them, a process that is both time-consuming and messy.

PLASTIC LAMINATE INSTALLATION

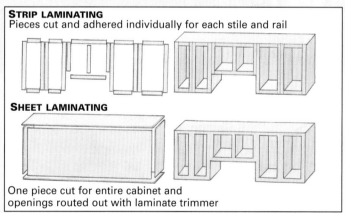

STRIP LAMINATING
Pieces cut and adhered individually for each stile and rail

SHEET LAMINATING

One piece cut for entire cabinet and openings routed out with laminate trimmer

You can apply plastic laminate either in strips or in sheets. Strip laminating means cutting individual pieces and adhering them to the frame. This method consumes less material but takes more time. Use vertical-grade stock when strip laminating—it cuts and applies easily.

To sheet-laminate, cut the material slightly oversize and glue it to the frame. Then, beginning at a starter hole, trim the openings with a laminate trimmer. This method results in more waste but takes less time and produces a seamless front. Horizontal-grade laminate comes in larger sheets—you may have to use it if you can't cover the front with a single vertical-grade sheet.

SELECTING NEW CABINETS

All modern cabinet cases are made with a veneered substrate that resists warping.

Selecting new cabinets can be an adventure or a bewildering experience. The difference depends on how much time you spend familiarizing yourself with what's available. Depending on the number of cabinetry distributors in your area and your access to catalog and Internet suppliers, you should allow four to seven days for a comprehensive survey. But don't go shopping without arming yourself with some basic information about cabinet construction, stock features, custom options, and techniques for judging quality.

HOW CABINETS ARE MADE

Cabinets are constructed in two types—framed and frameless. Until the late 1940s, all cabinets on this continent were framed—their fronts were faced with narrow pieces that hid the edges of the case and defined each door and drawer opening. Doors were hinged to the frame members.

The need for low-cost, lumber-conserving construction in Europe after World War II led to the frameless cabinet—a box shell with doors, attached by hidden hinges, covering the edges.

Until recently, you could tell the difference between these two styles without opening the doors. With framed construction, you could see the frames at the door edges; with frameless cabinets, you could not. Modern construction techniques have minimized differences in appearance.

Frameless cabinets, however, offer two practical advantages: Interior access is easier without the frame, and the countertop height can vary because some boxes are built to rest on separate plinths, or pedestals.

Plywood

Medium-Density Fiberboard (MDF)

Particleboard

TYPICAL CABINET CONSTRUCTION

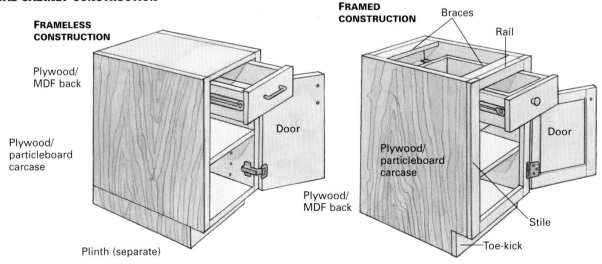

FRAMELESS CONSTRUCTION

Plywood/MDF back

Plywood/particleboard carcase

Door

Plinth (separate)

FRAMED CONSTRUCTION

Braces

Rail

Plywood/particleboard carcase

Plywood/MDF back

Door

Stile

Toe-kick

DESIGNING WITH STAINLESS

Once almost entirely limited to commercial kitchens, stainless steel is rapidly migrating into domestic kitchens. Use it to define a sleek, contemporary, or high-tech decor or on countertops and wheeled carts to accent a Bauhaus design.

On cabinets, you'll find it either with or without a wood core. Those made with a core won't sound tinny when doors and drawers are opened and closed.

Stainless-steel countertops provide a hard, durable surface that doesn't absorb spills. It is easy to clean and resists the formation of bacteria. Perhaps its only maintenance drawbacks are that it tends to show scratches and fingerprints and it dents.

With its increased popularity, some manufacturers are producing custom-made stainless countertops, both with and without backsplashes. A few do business on the Internet. Order the countertop to the dimensions of your cabinets. Countertops come ready to screw down to the corner blocks in the frame.

READY TO ASSEMBLE

Ready-to-assemble (RTA) cabinetry is a relatively recent addition to stock cabinet styles.

Ordering procedures vary from company to company but almost always involve providing a sketch with measurements and model numbers for the style you have chosen from the manufacturer's catalog.

The manufacturer ships all the cabinetry pieces—including hardware, hinges, and fasteners—to you unassembled, along with instructions. You provide the labor for assembly.

The selection from some distributors is small; others offer solid wood, thermal foil, laminate, and polyester-clad doors and drawer fronts.

Because you are not paying for labor costs, RTA units are substantially less expensive than other stock cabinetry. Many distributors do business over the Internet, and some will even supply you with blank grids on which you can draw your cabinet layout.

In both styles, the cabinet box or case is usually made of plywood, particleboard, or medium-density fiberboard (MDF). The less attractive sheet materials can be used because the case is faced with veneer or laminate, depending on the style and the materials of the doors and drawer fronts. Frames and drawer fronts for veneered cabinets are usually made from solid wood. In laminate-covered cabinets, the cores of the doors and drawer fronts are usually made of the same materials as the box. Face frames for framed cabinets are usually made of solid wood.

WOOD FINISHES

Regardless of how a cabinet is made, the price reflects the type of finish applied. Synthetic materials, such as laminates and RTF, require no additional finish, and their cost is usually lower than that for cabinets made of wood and separately finished.

The finish for most wood units begins with application of stain to give the wood a uniform color, followed by several coats of clear finish, which adds depth and luster and protects the wood. Polyurethane finishes are remarkably durable, adding a protective plastic coating to the wood surface. Catalyzed varnishes are even tougher, and their cost is

higher. If you buy unfinished cabinets or build your own, refer to the chart on page 17 for help in determining the appropriate finish.

FROM STOCK TO CUSTOM

Both frameless and framed cabinets are available in stock, semi-custom, and custom designs. Here are the distinctions:

STOCK CABINETS are preassembled and offer consistent quality at usually (but not always) lower cost than semi-custom or custom varieties. These are the cabinets on display at your local home center. Cabinet sizes are standard, but the range of sizes is large enough to meet most needs. You won't get as much choice in style as you might with other kinds of cabinets, but you probably won't have to wait long for delivery. Some centers offer same-day pickup, and many will provide you with a complete range of design services if you purchase the units from them. There's a wide variety of specialized units available in these lines too. You can order lazy Susans, pantries with swing-out doors, slide-out breadboards, open shelving, and more.

SELECTING NEW CABINETS
continued

Plan your new cabinets to provide adequate storage and easy access. Pots, pans, and lids are easier to get to in this drawer than on shelves.

SEMI-CUSTOM manufacturers usually make a larger number of styles than most retail outlets stock. These styles are available by special order. The manufacturer's range of materials may be smaller than what's available at large home centers, but within that range, you'll find extensive options in door styles, finishes, and features. You will have more choices, but delivery time will be longer. Semi-custom units do not come from stock and may take several weeks to arrive.

CUSTOM CABINETS are built from the ground up, tailored specifically to your location and desires. Expect the highest quality in materials and construction here, as well as a considerable increase in cost. These cabinets are made one at a time, which means that a skilled cabinetmaker will come to your home, measure the installation, and build the cabinets to your specifications. If you are adding a new run or unit to an existing style which is no longer available from dealers, custom cabinets are the only option. Consider ordering your cabinets in combined units— a single run of 8 feet can save time and some of the expense of installation over the cost of individual cabinets. Make sure you can get it into the house, though. Cabinetmakers are not always designers. For extensive installations or renovations, hire a design consultant. Turnaround time for custom cabinets is at least five to eight weeks.

CHECKING FOR QUALITY

Make the drawers your first step in judging the quality of cabinets. Pull the drawer out about ½ inch; if it closes by itself, that's a good sign. Then pull it out all the way— it should stop before it falls out, although you should make sure that you can easily remove

GUIDE TO SELECTING CABINETS

STOCK CABINETS
■ Wide choice of styles and materials available in local home centers.
■ Materials will often meet only minimum quality standards. Watch for mismatched elements, inferior woods, and poor construction. Avoid stapled construction.
■ Style and choice of options often limited to showroom or catalog selections.
■ Sales staff knowledge of design and material options may be limited to the basics.
■ Lower cost than custom and semi-custom cabinets, but prices are still substantial.
■ Minimum delivery time. Sometimes same-day pickup.
■ Installation not included. Some outlets will arrange installation.

SEMI-CUSTOM CABINETS
■ Wide variety of style choices available for viewing in showrooms and sometimes in catalogs.
■ Generally higher-quality materials and construction methods. Cabinet box usually of medium-density fiberboard. Laminates and catalyzed varnishes are durable.
■ Wide selection of cabinet sizes, specialty units (corner cabinets and pantries), and options available.
■ Sales staff usually well-trained and knowledgeable about design and material options.
■ Cost will be higher than stock, but less than custom cabinetry, more if you request kitchen design help.
■ Five to eight weeks delivery time, sometimes longer, depending on options selected.
■ Price usually includes installation.

CUSTOM CABINETS
■ Somewhat limited style options available and usually viewable only in pictures or catalogs.
■ Material quality subject to your specifications. Quality of workmanship usually high. Check installations in other homes to accurately assess workmanship.
■ Sizes built to order in a vast range. Options are likely to be somewhat limited.
■ Cabinetmaker is probably the salesperson, may know much about materials, less about style.
■ Very wide range of costs, but usually higher than stock or semi-custom manufacture.
■ A minimum five to eight weeks delivery time, depending on number of options and level of detail.
■ Price often includes installation.

the drawer for cleaning. The drawer should release easily and should be easy to put back in place too.

Next, examine the corners of the drawers. Dovetailed or doweled joints are signs of high-quality construction. Drawers fastened together with staples will not be durable. The drawer bottom should be about 3/8 inch thick, to keep it from sagging under heavy loads. The bottom should fit into dadoes (grooves) cut into the drawer sides.

Then look at the finished cabinet surface. On wood cabinets, the grain and color of the cabinet veneers should closely match the doors and drawers. Unless you want a definite rustic look, avoid knots or blemishes. Look for tight joints, square corners, smoothly rounded exposed edges, and doors that hang straight and swing properly.

Examine the edges of plastic laminate. There should be no voids where one laminate face meets another. Voids mean that one surface, usually the edging, will come loose with use.

Check door construction too. Surfaces should be perfectly flat and should not show scratches across the joints of solid-wood frames. Inset panels or glass panes should not rattle. Tap them with your knuckles to check them. In a home entertainment center, loose panels can resonate with the sounds coming from your speakers. Make sure the doors fit the openings without gaps or binding.

Incorporate custom touches like this pull-out breadboard into your new plan for more convenience and utility.

Ask about the kind of finish material and the number of coats applied. More are usually better. The finish should feel smooth and satiny, not rough and gritty. Poor finishes will not take spills without damage and will be damaged by even gentle cleaning.

Finally, if you're shopping for kitchen cabinets, look for the Kitchen Cabinet Manufacturers Association (KCMA) seal. It certifies that all aspects of the unit—from materials to hinges—meet the association's minimum standards.

ISLANDS

Islands can enhance the livability of many rooms in the house. In a kitchen, an island adds another food preparation surface and can be used for dining. In a family room, an island can divide activity areas from reading and relaxing areas. And in an office, an island is perfect for adding storage or work surface combinations.

Islands need surrounding space to work well, however. Crammed into a too-small area, they become obstacles instead of improvements. Allow 30 to 42 inches on at least three sides; 33 inches minimum unless the space is used primarily as a passageway.

To make sure you're not encumbering the room, tape an outline of your proposed island on the floor or put cardboard of the island size on a stool. Keep the tape or cardboard in place for several days; walk around it to get used to it. If you feel uncomfortable with it, reduce the size of the island or abandon the idea altogether.

SIZING THINGS UP

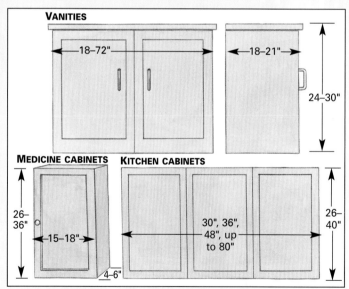

Cabinets come in a standard range of sizes that you can combine into virtually any layout.

Shown above are standard sizes that you'll find in most home centers. Some home centers, cabinet dealers, and catalog and Internet suppliers will offer more sizes than the standard sizes shown. Custom cabinets, of course, are made to fit and can be ordered in any size.

PULLS, HINGES, AND DRAWER SLIDES

Cabinet hardware provides more than a means of opening and closing doors and drawers. Knobs, pulls, and the exposed portions of hinges are decorative elements as well, and can make the difference between a ho-hum installation and one that gets rave reviews.

BLEND IN OR ACCENT?

One of the first things to decide is whether you want to downplay the hardware and make it almost invisible or let it stand out and serve as a style element itself. This decision applies principally to pulls and knobs, but will affect your choice of hinges too.

There is no single rule to guide you in hardware selection except your own taste. If you replace hardware and hinges on existing doors and drawer fronts, remember that hardware with mountings that are spaced differently as on the existing hardware will require new mounting holes. Unless the new hardware covers them, the old holes will show, no matter how well you try to fill them. Unless you paint the cabinets (which will hide the patched holes), it's better to replace the doors and drawer fronts or find hardware that will mount in or cover the old holes.

KNOBS AND PULLS

Hardware stores, home centers, and cabinet dealers carry an extraordinary range of knobs and pulls made from plastic, metal, wood, ceramic, and combinations of these materials. Knobs are generally round or rectangular and mounted with one fastener. Pulls are mounted with two fasteners, except pendants and rings, which have one screw. There are matching sets of knobs and pulls. You also can find invisible openers—latches combined with push-and-release mechanisms that spring the doors open at a touch.

Whatever you choose, let your sense of style and personal taste guide you. Consider the overall look you want from your cabinets, then select knobs and pulls that fit your style. A single brass knob on a plain, flush door will create a Shaker or traditional look. A brushed chrome or stainless-steel pull on the same door will look more contemporary.

Consider installing backer plates that mount under knobs or pulls. The slightly higher cost can be paid back over time by reducing damage to the finish caused by constant contact with fingers and fingernails.

CENTER-MOUNT DRAWER SLIDE

KNOBS AND PULLS

SIDE-MOUNT DRAWER SLIDE WITH BALL BEARINGS

DECORATIVE AND INVISIBLE HINGES

THE EURO PULL

For a classic Eurostyle cabinet nothing beats the Euro pull (also called a continuous wood pull). This strip of finished wood with a routed recess mounts across doors and drawer fronts and imparts a clean, contemporary flair to plastic laminate cabinets. The pulls are available in a number of different woods, stains, and finishes. The color and grain of red oak contributes an appealing contrast to monochrome white or beige laminate cabinet fronts.

HINGES

The overlay of your cabinet doors (see "Door Overlays" on page 14) limits your choice of hinges. Mount inset doors with surface hinges, butt hinges, or wraparound hinges. The latter two types require mortising the edge of the face frame and the door. Rabbeted doors are usually hung with lipped (sometimes called semi-inset) hinges. Overlay doors are best mounted with hidden Eurostyle hinges. Within these categories there is almost as much variety as with knobs and pulls. In general, if any part of the hinge is visible, its style and appearance should complement the style of the knob or pull. Most hinges are available in a variety of finishes.

DRAWER SLIDES

Drawer slides serve two functions: They keep the drawer centered in its opening and prevent the drawer from tipping or falling out when it's opened more than halfway. Drawer slides are rated for weight capacity; opt for a high rating for kitchen drawers.

Side-mounted slides attach to each side of the drawer. Center-mounted slides have one guide rail that attaches to the back of the cabinet face frame and the rear of the cabinet. They are less expensive than side-mounted slides, but provide less support.

If you're refacing your cabinets and plan to keep the old drawer boxes, you should upgrade the slides. Side-mounted ball-bearing slides will outperform and outlast others. Self-closing slides are also handy, especially for busy cooks and in compact bathrooms.

HINGE STYLES AND CHARACTERISTICS

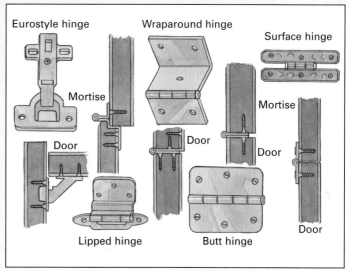

Each style of hinge mounts in a particular way. Pick hinges that work with your door overlay, and be sure exposed or partially exposed hinges contribute to the look you want.

■ **SURFACE HINGES** go well with many country and period decors. They are inexpensive and mount easily, but can't be adjusted. They require a latch to keep the door closed.

■ **BUTT HINGES** are appropriate to period cabinet styles, but will not work well on inset doors. They are inexpensive (except for solid brass), but require a mortise in the cabinet and door and are difficult to adjust. Doors need separate latches or catches.

■ **WRAPAROUND HINGES** have an extra flange inside the door to provide additional support for heavy inset doors. They require door and cabinet mortises. Moderately expensive, they are difficult to adjust and require latches.

■ **LIPPED HINGES** for rabbeted doors work well with any style in which a visible hinge pin is acceptable. They are easy to mount and not costly. Some are self-closing. They're difficult to adjust.

■ **EUROSTYLE HINGES** are the standard for full overlay doors. There are styles to suit other door types. They fit a 35mm hole in the door, adjust in three planes, and are self-closing. Most are moderately priced, but specialty models are expensive.

ACCESSORIES

Installing new cabinets—or just refacing existing units—presents opportunities for improving convenience. Consider the options below to increase the comfort, ease of use, and organization of your cabinets. They will also work in your office or family room.

■ Roll-out or swing-out shelves
■ Slide-out wire baskets and bins
■ Cutlery and utensil dividers
■ Tilt panels for sink fronts
■ Lazy Susans for corner access
■ Open shelving for decorative accents

LATCHES AND CATCHES

Doors need latches to keep them closed. Surface-mounted brass or wrought-iron catches work well for a country or rustic look. Friction devices or magnetic latches that fit inside the cabinet are good for traditional or contemporary styles. Self-closing hinges keep doors closed without catches. But self-closing models that go with country and period styles can be hard to find.

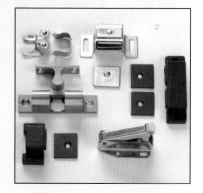

COUNTERTOP SURFACES

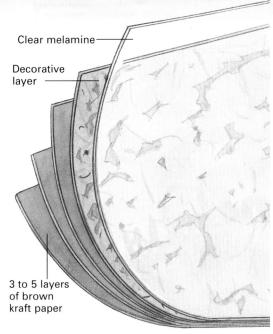

Clear melamine

Decorative layer

3 to 5 layers of brown kraft paper

Its wide range of colors and textures and low cost make plastic laminate an attractive countertop choice. Laminate is tough and easy to clean, but it is subject to chipping and is difficult to repair.

Countertops are subjected to constant wear and tear, so even if you have no plans to replace your cabinets, you may want a new countertop. The first step in replacing a drab or worn-out countertop is to decide on a material. To make your selection a little easier, look for materials that will match the overall style of the room, and consider both how much abuse it can take and how easy it is to maintain. Then see if your choices fit into your budget.

at home centers will help you get information a little at a time, and you won't feel overwhelmed. From there, you can turn to catalogs, mail-order outlets, and local specialty firms. Find local retailers in the Yellow Pages under "Countertops," "Kitchens," or "Cabinets." For ceramic tile, concrete, and stone, check listings under those subjects. Designers and architects may also stock samples. You'll find the full range of materials from which you can make your final choice at these outlets and by checking Internet websites.

SHOPPING FOR COUNTERTOPS

Start shopping in your local home center. Outlets specializing in home decorating carry a limited range of materials, usually plastic laminates and solid-surface products. Some may display tile and wood countertops, but all will have limited selections of each. Starting

COMPARING COUNTERTOP COST

Material	Price per running foot, installed
Plastic laminate	$25–75
Ceramic tile	$35–75
Wood	$35–100
Concrete	$110–200
Solid-surface material	$140–250
Stainless steel	$150–250
Granite and marble	$200–250

Prices of materials and installation vary widely from region to region and from manufacturer to manufacturer. The ranges shown above should be taken as rough estimates only, intended to indicate general relationships between categories of materials. Expect to pay one-third to one-half less if doing the work yourself.

INSTALLING COUNTERTOPS

Each type of countertop material requires different installation methods, a factor that might influence your decision about which to install. Here's a brief review on installation for each material.

■ **PLASTIC LAMINATE:** Install a new particleboard base. Then cut, adhere, and trim laminate sheets and strips. For post-formed countertops, cut to length and attach to cabinets.

■ **CERAMIC TILE:** Install a new plywood base, cut and attach cement backerboard, trowel on adhesive, lay tile, and grout.

■ **WOOD:** Cut and screw ready-to-install sections to corner blocks in cabinet frame.

■ **SOLID-SURFACE MATERIAL:** Usually must be built and installed by a trained fabricator to be covered by warranty.

■ **STAINLESS STEEL:** Order sections to fit, attach with screws to corner blocks.

■ **GRANITE AND MARBLE:** Hire a professional installer.

PLASTIC LAMINATE

Plastic laminates are formed from thin plastic-impregnated kraft paper sheets bonded together under heat and pressure. (See the illustration on the opposite page.) Manufactured in a wide variety of colors, textures, and patterns, laminates fit almost any decor. The low cost of laminates can be especially attractive for homeowners on a tight budget.

Laminates resist stains and are durable and easy to clean, but they scratch and chip, especially at the edges. Hot pots or pans can mar the surface without a heat-resistant pad. The brown edge shows, which may distract from your design. Make sure you purchase horizontal-grade laminate—it's thicker and made specifically for countertops.

CERAMIC TILE

Tile is a favorite countertop material because it stands up to hard use and is easy to clean. Colors and patterns are virtually unlimited. Unglazed tile is porous and requires sealing, as do grout joints, to prevent stains. Tile is brittle and will chip. Because each piece is laid individually, a tiled countertop can be customized with patterns or by putting in accent or decorative tiles. Make sure to buy tile suited for horizontal surfaces (some floor tiles make good countertop surfaces). Buy all the tile at once, and purchase trim tile from the same manufacturer.

MORE THAN ONE MATERIAL?

For the ideal countertop, take advantage of the different properties of materials by mixing them.

Use stainless steel around the sink for easy cleanup; stainless steel, ceramic tile, or granite (not marble or other stone) near the stove or cooktops for hot pans. Install drop-in butcher-block sections for cutting and carving that pop out when they need to be cleaned and sealed. Build one granite section 30 inches high for rolling pastries.

Mixing materials can spice up the looks of your kitchen too. Tile or wood on the backsplash offers a sharp contrast to a plastic laminate countertop.

Tile is available in more colors and shapes than perhaps any other material, and it's heat- and water-resistant. Properly installed tile is virtually indestructible.

Solid-surface material, at about the midpoint in the material price range, offers two advantages: Its colors go through the material, and its surface doesn't show seams.

Marble and granite countertops look elegant—at a price. Both are best installed professionally. Here they are combined with a wood cutting surface.

Marble

Wood

Granite

COUNTERTOP SURFACES
continued

WOOD

Long a favorite for country and vintage looks, wood is sturdy and long lasting. But it's softer than other materials and is subject to scratches, burns, and wear. Maple butcher block is a popular wood countertop, but other woods—such as cherry, white oak, and teak—make good choices too.

Wood must be treated and sealed for countertop use. Satin polyurethanes or catalyzed varnishes will minimize wear and staining in both bathroom vanities and kitchens, but oil finishes are often used in kitchens where nicks and scratches are likely. Consider installing wood sections with other materials for an attractive design alternative.

SOLID-SURFACE MATERIAL

Solid-surface materials are polymer plastics mixed with particulates and colorants cast in continuous sheets. Some varieties are made to look like marble, granite, and other stone. Short countertop runs are installed in one piece. Long runs or L-shapes are seamed, but the finishing process hides the seams. Solid-surface tops come with or without backsplashes and can be ordered with precast sinks, an attractive option both for design and ease of installation.

Because their coloring goes clear through, solid-surface products wear well. Scratches can usually be polished out. Installation is not difficult, but most manufacturers require professional installation.

STONE

Marble and granite are popular choices in stone countertops, followed by limestone and slate. Stone fits both formal and informal designs, and is perfect for vanities and dining room sideboard serving centers too.

Granite is the toughest of the stones and will stand up to chopping, pastry rolling, hot

Wood immediately conjures up warm feelings. Maple butcher block, edge-glued in strips, is the most popular wood countertop material. Other hardwoods, such as the cherry, shown here, are decorative and functional.

Concrete offers more variety in style than you might imagine. It can be colored to match any decorating scheme, formed and shaped into contours not possible with other materials, and if properly installed, will give years of service.

CULTURED MARBLE

Cultured marble is a man-made product that technically falls into the category of cast-polymer (solid-surface) materials. Like other solid-surface products, it is made from polyester resins mixed with inorganic particles and coloring agents, then molded to shape. Some cultured marble mixtures contain ground-up marble dust or limestone. Others add chemical compounds that simulate the appearance of marble, granite, and onyx.

You may find differences in quality and price from one manufacturer to another. These materials usually have a gel-coat surface, which scratches easily and cannot be repaired.

pots, and utensil abuse better than marble. Food acids discolor marble and limestone, so they must be resealed annually. Granite is less porous, and certain types need resealing, although less frequently than marble.

Stone works well with other materials—for example, a marble section can be installed for pastry preparation. Such installations may require shimming to even out the difference in top thicknesses. Nature does not produce stone in consistent color lots, so you should examine your purchase before it is delivered. Make sure any color differences from piece to piece are acceptable. A stone slab countertop is best installed by professionals. Thinner stone tile is reasonably priced and uniformly sized for easy installation by any homeowner with moderate skills.

Manufactured granite, made from crushed granite, epoxy resin, and colorants, is a good alternative. It is harder than granite, impervious to stains, and comes with a 10-year warranty. Manufactured granite can overhang a cabinet edge by up to twice as far as natural stone.

CONCRETE

Concrete, a mixture of portland cement, aggregate, and water, is a relatively new countertop material for American kitchens. It has been used on countertops in countries south of the American border for years.

The high-density concrete used for countertops is strong, easily shaped and colored, and can be precast or poured on site. It resists scratches and heat, but stains easily. Stains can be checked by applying lacquer sealer. If not properly prepared and cured, concrete will crack. Because pouring, finishing, and proper curing require special skills, concrete should be installed by a pro.

STAINLESS STEEL

Stainless steel has long been a standard countertop material in commercial kitchens, laboratories, and hospitals because it resists stains, shrugs off heat, doesn't harbor bacteria, and cleans easily.

Its stark look has kept it out of residential settings, but it's becoming more popular for its high-tech look. It's also used for its functional value in kitchens and bathrooms. Wood, stone, and other materials are often added to temper the industrial look.

Not all stainless steel is equal. Material thinner than 16 gauge dents easily. Look for a numerical series designation, an indication of the grade and composition of the steel. Stainless steel with numbers in the 300 range is often used for culinary equipment.

Stainless steel is waterproof, heat-resistant, and easy to maintain. But it is impractical as a cutting surface, and polished stainless steel shows scratches and dents. To keep the cost down, install prefabricated sections for an island or workstation.

COMPARISON OF COUNTERTOP MATERIALS

	Stain / Heat / Scratch Resistance	Maintenance	Cost
Plastic laminate	High / Low / Low	Difficult to repair	Least expensive
Ceramic tile	High / High / High	Broken tile can be removed and replaced	Inexpensive to expensive, depending on quality
Wood	Low / Low / Moderate	Sand scratches, seal with mineral oil	Inexpensive to expensive, depending on species
Concrete	Low / High / Low	Difficult to repair	Moderate
Solid surface	High / Moderate / Low	Sand scratches and blemishes	Moderate
Stainless steel	High / High / Moderate	Seldom needs repair	Expensive
Stone	High / High / High	Difficult to repair	Very expensive

Put all of your design ideas and cabinet layouts on paper before installing new units or refacing them. You'll need graph paper, *a couple of sharp pencils, and a ruler to get started. Templates—available from cabinet dealers—will make your layout drawing more precise.*

DO IT YOURSELF OR CONTRACT IT?

Doing it yourself can save one-third to one-half of the overall costs of refacing old cabinets or installing new ones. But time constraints and other factors may mean that hiring a contractor to do the renovation makes more sense.

Start looking for a reliable contractor by asking friends for recommendations. Contact at least three contractors and tell them you are seeking bids for the work. In order to get an accurate bid, have copies of your dimensioned plan ready for contractors to study. Ask the contractors for references so you can check the quality of their work.

Review each bid carefully. Be wary of bids that are substantially lower than the average of the others. Choose the contractor that will give you the best value for the cost—not necessarily the one who offers the lowest bid.

PLANNING

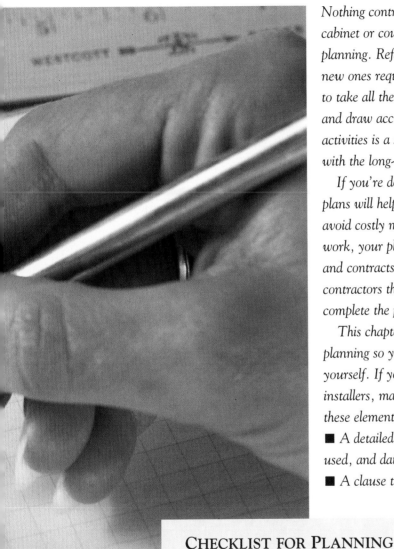

Nothing contributes more to the success of a cabinet or countertop installation than careful planning. Refacing old cabinets or installing new ones requires attention to detail, so be sure to take all the time you need to measure layouts and draw accurate plans. Time spent for these activities is a small consideration, compared with the long-term rewards you'll reap.

If you're doing the job yourself, detailed plans will help you stay within your budget and avoid costly mistakes. If you're contracting the work, your plans will serve as the basis for bids and contracts and will give suppliers and contractors the information they need to complete the project successfully.

This chapter covers the essential steps in planning so you can complete the work yourself. If you decide to hire professional installers, make sure your contract contains these elements:

■ A detailed description of the work, materials used, and dates of completion for each step.

■ A clause that lets you back out if you change your mind—usually restricted to three days after signing the contract.

■ The name of the contractor's bonding agency and insurance carrier.

■ A warranty covering workmanship and material quality for at least a year.

■ Mechanic's lien waivers to protect you from liens by subcontractors if the contractor defaults.

CHECKLIST FOR PLANNING

Use this checklist to organize your planning.
■ Measure the cabinet wall and individual units carefully.
■ Create a scaled drawing with dimensions.
■ Using the area of the cabinet surfaces or individual unit measurements, prepare a materials list and estimate quantities.
■ Prepare and submit material orders, and make note of delivery dates.
■ Plan adequate storage of materials, allowing sufficient time for them to acclimate to conditions in your home.
■ Prepare a calendar that includes your construction schedule and contract specifications.

SIZING UP YOUR LAYOUT

STANDARD KITCHEN DIMENSIONS

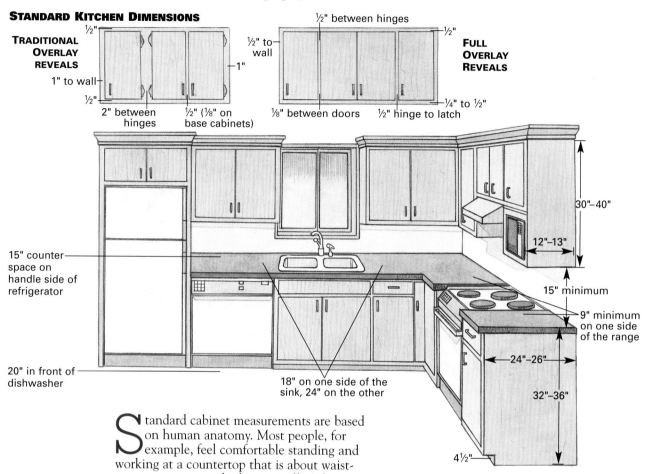

TRADITIONAL OVERLAY REVEALS

½"
½"
1" to wall
½"
2" between hinges
½" (⅛" on base cabinets)
1"

½" between hinges
½" to wall
½"
⅛" between doors
½" hinge to latch
¼" to ½"

FULL OVERLAY REVEALS

15" counter space on handle side of refrigerator

20" in front of dishwasher

18" on one side of the sink, 24" on the other

30"–40"

12"–13"

15" minimum

9" minimum on one side of the range

24"–26"

32"–36"

4½"

Standard cabinet measurements are based on human anatomy. Most people, for example, feel comfortable standing and working at a countertop that is about waist-high—typically 3 feet above floor level. For seated work, a surface 30 to 32 inches high feels right for most people. Wall cabinets provide the easiest access when located 15 to 18 inches above the countertops.

Remember, however, that these measurements and others illustrated on these pages are norms and averages. You can change them to make the installation more usable or comfortable for you—if you're taller or shorter than average, for instance.

and requirements are part of the Americans with Disabilities Act (ADA).

For wheelchair access, countertops must not be higher than 34 inches from the floor. Clearance under a sink must be 36 inches wide and 27 inches high. The maximum reach to a sink faucet should be 21 inches. Important storage units should be between 15 and 48 inches from the floor. To accommodate all members of the family, consider installing standard cabinets along with work areas and other sections with dimensions that meet these accessibility requirements. Keep in mind that the measurements noted above are maximums—the comfort and convenience of the user may dictate lower or shallower cabinets and countertops.

BUILDING CODES

Local authorities establish building codes to set standards for construction safety and quality. Although these codes are usually based on a national standard, requirements can vary widely from community to community.

None of the individual projects described in this book is likely to require clearance from local code officials. But the projects might require plans, permits, and inspections if they are part of a total remodeling project. Some communities require that an entire plumbing system be upgraded if only one change is made to it. To be safe, check with your local building department before you start any remodeling project.

ACCESSIBLE DESIGN

Designing for special accessibility calls for specific changes in standard dimensions. Accessibility standards

MEASURE FOR CONVENIENCE

If you often think of your kitchen or bath as inconvenient or impractical, altering the amount of cabinet space may be the remedy.
■ For a kitchen less than 150 square feet, plan at least 144 inches of cabinet frontage (the total width of all cabinets combined).

■ For larger kitchens, plan a minimum of 186 inches of frontage.

■ Assuming an average depth of 12 inches and a 30-inch height for wall cabinets, plan to install at least 60 inches of frontage.

■ Don't skimp on countertop space at the sink. Try to allow 24 inches of open space on one side and 18 inches on the other. And if you prepare food beside the sink, provide 36 inches on that side.

■ To save a lot of steps across the room, have 15 inches of countertop space as a staging area on at least one side of the microwave oven and on the latch side of the refrigerator.

■ For eating areas on countertops and islands, allow a 12×24-inch space for each person. Leave 36 inches from the edge of the dining surface to the back wall or from any other obstacle—other cabinets, for example.

■ Drop the countertop to 30–32 inches for a pastry workstation to make rolling piecrusts and kneading dough easier. Test with a table to find the ideal height.

■ Design inside corners so doors and drawers don't hit each other. Use a true corner cabinet if possible.

■ Locate your new vanity out of the traffic

PLAN FOR SAFETY

While you have the pencils and paper out, build some safety features into your installation.

■ Round off sharp corners of islands and peninsulas to reduce cuts and scrapes.

■ Store things that can be harmful to children in wall cabinets.

■ Locate microwave and wall ovens so that hot spills won't fall from overhead.

■ Replace standard electrical outlets with ground fault circuit interrupters (GFCIs).

■ Include an area next to the stove so you can set hot items down safely before moving them to other places.

■ Put self-closing hinges on cabinet doors and self-closing slides on drawers.

■ Plan refrigerator and oven locations so their doors don't swing into natural traffic patterns.

pattern in the bath, with at least 21 inches in front of it and 15 inches between its centerline and any side wall or the toilet.

■ Allow 30 inches between two lavatory bowls. Most prefabricated units will come that way; some custom units may not.

WHILE YOU'RE AT IT

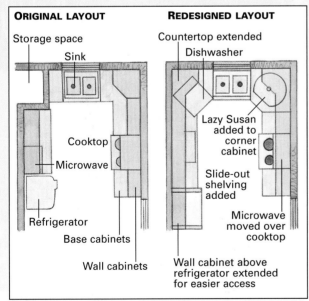

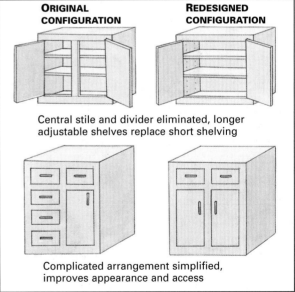

Central stile and divider eliminated, longer adjustable shelves replace short shelving

Complicated arrangement simplified, improves appearance and access

Refacing your existing cabinets offers an opportunity to redesign some aspects of your kitchen. Sometimes only a few changes can make a kitchen layout remarkably more efficient.

In the illustration above left, a hard-to-get-to corner unit was replaced with a lazy Susan and utility space in an adjoining room was modified to accommodate a dishwasher. New tilt trays under the sink now keep

dishwashing tools out of sight and out of the way. Extending the wall cabinet above the refrigerator made previously unused storage space more accessible.

If you don't need such drastic changes, simplify your face frames. Eliminating a central stile and making wider shelves gives you more room and easier access. Combine drawers into single-door storage. Add sliding shelves, adjustable shelf supports, and sliding trash bins.

PUTTING YOUR PLANS ON PAPER

TYPICAL DIMENSIONED DRAWING, KITCHEN

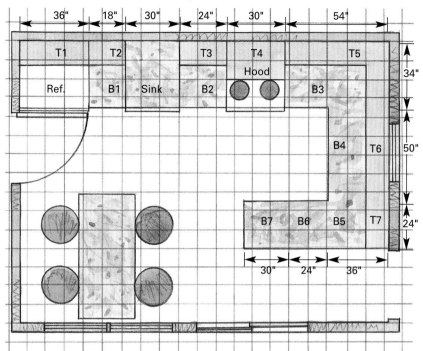

conditions; actual coverage is usually a little less than that.

MEASURE FOR REFACING

Draw each wall that has cabinets. Start by measuring the length and height of each wall. Outline each wall to scale on graph paper with a ¼-inch grid so it's easy to read. Mark the height to soffits, if they will remain in your new installation.

■ DRAWING IN THE CABINETS: Next, measure the total length and height of the wall cabinets and draw them on the wall drawing. Post the dimensions as you go. Do the same for the base cabinets. Now go back and measure and draw each individual cabinet in both the top and bottom runs. Be sure to measure the cabinets, not the doors. Add the individual measurements together. If they don't equal the length of the run, measure again and change the notations on your drawing.

■ DOORS AND DRAWER FRONTS: Now measure the doors and drawer fronts and add them to the drawing. If your cabinets are fairly new and you're not changing the amount of door overlay, you can use the existing measurements. For other installations, or if you are modifying the overlay, sketch the doors and subtract the combined amount of the reveals from the width of the cabinet. For example, to achieve a 1-inch reveal on both sides of a door on an 18-inch-wide cabinet, you need a door 16 inches wide. Reveals are not always the same all around; measure them all. Compute the door heights and the drawer fronts the same way and note all the measurements on your drawing. Make comparable doors the same height. Order new doors using these dimensions, specifying the width first and then the length. Door manufacturers work with ¹⁄₁₆-inch tolerance, so you can round your measurements up or down to the nearest ¹⁄₁₆ inch and your new doors will fit.

■ ESTIMATING LAMINATE SHEETS: To order 2×8-foot laminate sheets for the face frames, divide the total number of openings by 10 and round up the result. So, in an installation with 15 door and drawer openings, you would need to purchase two sheets of laminate (¹⁵⁄₁₀=1½, rounded to 2). This method will allow you to cut face frame pieces oversize and trim them exactly.

Cabinet planning calls for precision. No cabinetry project is inexpensive; careful planning will help you get the best results from your investment in materials and time. A good plan will also help you estimate how much material you'll need.

Whether you are painting or refacing your cabinets, installing new units in a kitchen or bath, or planning a new cabinet wall for your family room or office, planning begins with accurate measurements.

For painting or refinishing you need to compute the surface area of the cabinets. If you're refacing the cabinets, you'll need to sketch a front view of them. And if you're ordering new cabinets or making your own, you should prepare a scaled top view of the layout and front and side views as necessary.

MEASURE FOR REFINISHING

Measure the length and height of the front and side surfaces (in inches) and write down the measurements. When you're finished, multiply the length by the width for each section, and add up the totals. Then divide the total (the surface area in square inches) by 144 to find the total surface area in square feet. Add about 5 percent to the total, then order paint or finish materials to cover that area. Most paint labels indicate that a gallon covers about 400 square feet based on ideal

PLANNING FOR NEW CABINETS

Measure the dimensions of your floor or the wall on which the cabinets will be located and transfer those dimensions to graph paper. Note the exact locations of plumbing fixtures that will come through the back of your cabinets and the exact locations of switches and outlets within the run.

■ **ADDING WINDOWS AND DOORS:** Place windows and doors to scale on the drawing. If you're drawing top views, you may find it easier to shade or number the wall cabinets rather than developing separate renderings for the wall and base cabinets.

■ **APPLIANCES NEXT:** Sketch in the location of various appliances— dishwasher, refrigerator, stove or wall oven in a kitchen; permanent fixtures in an office or family room; toilet, tub, and sink in a bath. Use templates scaled to your drawing to pencil in these features. Use tracing paper taped to the room layout drawing if you want to experiment with different arrangements.

When you have finalized the layout, it should look something like the one illustrated on the opposite page, with the cabinets labeled and measurements noted for each. The overhead views will give you a scaled representation of the position and dimensions of your new cabinets. You may also want to prepare a front elevation to make sure that the proportion of the cabinets looks exactly as you want it to.

Draw the outline of the wall on graph paper, then draw the outline of the base and wall cabinet runs corresponding to the locations established in the overhead view. Make sure your drawing shows the wall cabinets at the proper height and that the cabinet height is properly scaled. When you divide the cases into drawers and doors, you can match the upper units to the lower units or vice versa, or you can stagger the runs. Staggered designs look best when the edges of the top and bottom units are offset by at least one-fourth of the cabinet width. That way the offsets appear intentional, not accidental.

KITCHEN LAYOUT TIPS

The shape of your kitchen will affect its layout:

■ In a one-wall kitchen for a small area, install apartment-size appliances to maximize countertop space. Allow the minimum specified countertop space alongside the sink, range, and other appliances.

■ In a corridor kitchen, try to place sink and cooktop areas on opposite walls to allow plenty of side spaces.

■ L-shape kitchens lend themselves to comfortable work triangles. Put the refrigerator at one end of a cabinet run and the range at the other.

■ U-shape kitchens can have more work centers. They work best with at least 60 inches between the legs, 72 inches for a kitchen used by two cooks.

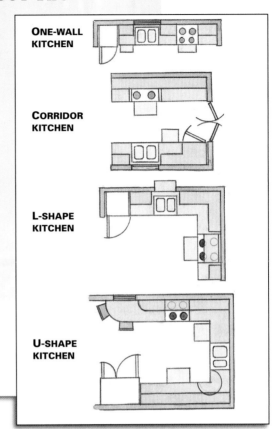

ONE-WALL KITCHEN

CORRIDOR KITCHEN

L-SHAPE KITCHEN

U-SHAPE KITCHEN

TAKING ACCURATE MEASUREMENTS

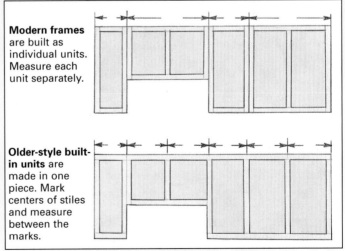

Modern frames are built as individual units. Measure each unit separately.

Older-style built-in units are made in one piece. Mark centers of stiles and measure between the marks.

Modern cabinets are built as individual units and fastened together in a run. To measure their widths, simply measure from one edge of the frame to the other.

To measure older cabinets installed with one continuous frame, divide the run into imaginary units, marking the centers of the exposed stiles and treating these marks as if they were the edges of individual face frames. Use these individual dimensions when figuring the width of new overlay doors.

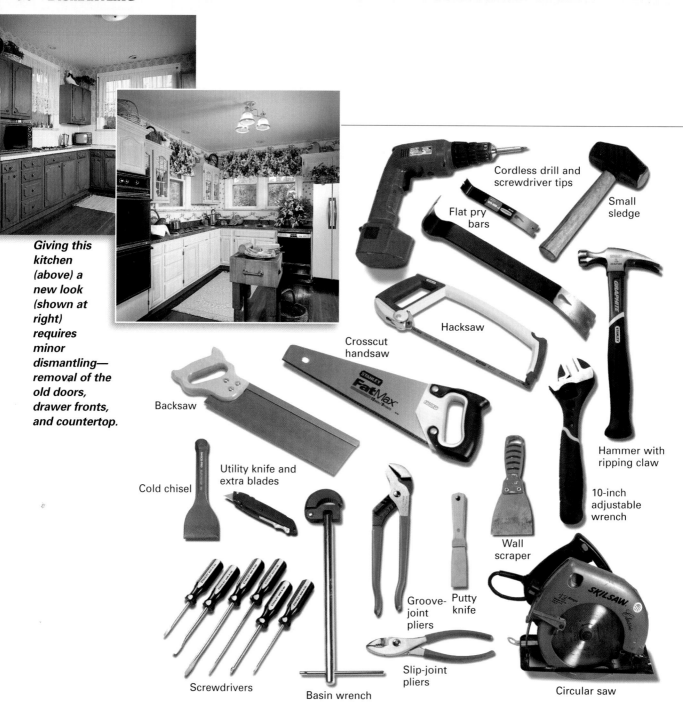

Giving this kitchen (above) a new look (shown at right) requires minor dismantling— removal of the old doors, drawer fronts, and countertop.

Cordless drill and screwdriver tips

Flat pry bars

Small sledge

Hacksaw

Crosscut handsaw

Backsaw

Hammer with ripping claw

Cold chisel

Utility knife and extra blades

10-inch adjustable wrench

Wall scraper

Groove-joint pliers

Putty knife

Screwdrivers

Slip-joint pliers

Basin wrench

Circular saw

MAKE A TEMPORARY KITCHEN

Removing and replacing your kitchen cabinets can disrupt more than the room itself. It can alter the family schedule and scramble your domestic routine. To keep inconvenience to a minimum, find a space you can use as a temporary kitchen—perhaps in your family room, dining room, or even your laundry room.

■ Set up temporary counter space on a table or other work area. Place the refrigerator close by.

■ Minimize utensil use. Paper plates and plastic dinnerware and cups will get you through the process with a minimum of cleaning.

■ Eat out or order take-out meals periodically if your budget will allow.

■ Use space-saving appliances— microwave, hot plate, and toaster oven. Rely on packaged food. In good weather, barbecue and have outdoor picnics.

■ Pack up everything that was in the cabinets and label the boxes. Move the boxes to another room so they don't interfere with your work.

■ If your temporary kitchen doesn't have its own sink, use two large plastic dishpans for washing.

DISMANTLING

Dismantling cabinetry requires planning, caution, and time more than brute force and heavy tools. If you're putting in a new countertop or replacing the cabinets, the old countertop and cabinetry must come out. If you're painting the cabinets or refacing them, leave them in place but remove the appliances so they don't become obstructions.

Your dismantling should roughly follow this order: Remove appliances and fixtures first (including a drop-in range and the sink), then the countertops, then the cabinetry. Some of these jobs will require various preliminary steps. You'll have to shut off the gas valve and remove the flex line before taking out a gas stove or a drop-in gas cooktop, for example. To remove a sink or dishwasher, shut off the water supply valves and disconnect the trap or drain lines.

If your cooking appliances are electric, you should unplug them. If you don't see a plug, they are wired directly into the circuit. For directly wired units, turn off the power at the breaker in the main service panel. Tape the breaker so someone in your household doesn't turn it on accidentally. After you have disconnected the wiring in the junction box, cap off the wires with wire nuts.

Tape plastic sheets over open doorways and keep the rest of the doors shut to keep dust out of the rest of the house. Remove trash and debris as you work so it doesn't become a safety hazard.

SAFETY FIRST

Removing wall cabinets poses a danger, especially if you're working by yourself. Get someone to help whenever possible. To keep the cabinets from falling off the wall as you remove the fasteners, support them with temporary bracing. Nail a ledger to the wall to support the rear of the cabinet and prop the front up with a 2×4.

Cabinet to be removed

Temporary ledger

2×4 prop

FOR ALL DISMANTLING CHORES, OBSERVE THESE SAFETY PRECAUTIONS.

■ Wear gloves, boots, a dust mask, and safety glasses.
■ Don't force things—let your tools do the work. If something proves stubborn, look for a fastener you missed.
■ Lift safely. Bend your legs, not your back. Keep your footing firm and avoid twisting motions.
■ Take nails out of boards as you go. Leaving them can lead to puncture wounds.

CLEAR OUT THE CAULK

Cabinets and vanities often have caulking around their edges. Some caulking compounds—especially old ones—can be stubborn when you try to remove them. Here are some tips that can make the job easier:
■ First, working slowly, scrape off the bulk of the caulk with a stiff putty knife.
■ Soften the remaining caulk with a commercial caulking remover.
Nonacrylic caulk will often come up with water, but you may need to soak it for several days. Some acrylic caulks will come up with rubbing alcohol. Silicone caulks are the hardest to remove. They can resist all chemical removers, but you may be able to get them down to an acceptable level with patient, careful scraping. Use a plastic scraper if working on a surface that sharp tools will damage easily, such as laminate.

REMOVING A COUNTERTOP

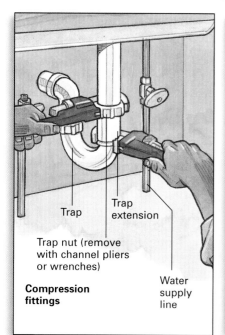

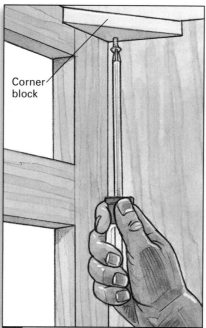

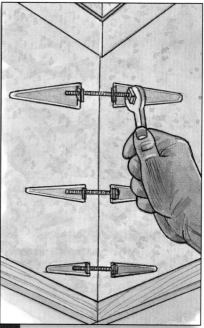

1 *Disconnect the water supply lines from the faucets and the trap from the sink. Disconnect the dishwasher drain hose and supply lines and any remaining plumbing fixtures. Shut off the power and gas and remove appliances.*

2 *Use a screwdriver or cordless drill and screwdriver bit to remove screws or brackets securing the countertop to the cabinet frame. Leave corner blocks and cabinet framing members in place.*

3 *If there is a mitered corner on a post-formed countertop, work underneath to unscrew the clamp bolts that join the corner. Remove the bolts completely and store them for use in reinstalling the countertop.*

REMOVING A TILE COUNTERTOP

Ceramic tile countertops are too heavy to lift and dispose of easily without first removing the tile. Using a cold chisel and heavy hammer, break up an edge tile and chip out the pieces to a grout joint. Insert a wide cold chisel under the edges of the tiles and pop them loose. If the tile is set on backerboard, you can remove the backerboard or leave it in place as you dismantle the countertop. If the tile is set in mortar, you'll have to cut it into pieces with a circular saw that has a masonry blade.

Removing a countertop appears perplexing at first because all the fasteners are hidden from view. Once you get under the countertop, however, dismantling will proceed quickly.

Even if you're not replacing your cabinets, you'll find that removing the countertop will go more smoothly if you take out the appliances. You must, of course, remove drop-in ranges and sinks. And pulling out other appliances, such as the dishwasher and trash compactor, will provide access to corner blocks or framing members. Getting the

TOOLBOX

REMOVING COUNTERTOP
- Open-end or adjustable wrenches or pump pliers
- Screwdriver or cordless drill
- Pry bar
- Utility knife

- Reciprocating saw (optional)

FOR TILE REMOVAL
- Cold chisel
- Large hammer
- Circular saw with masonry blade

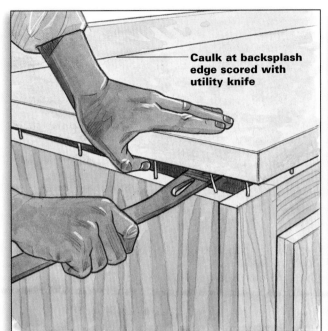

Caulk at backsplash
edge scored with
utility knife

4 To avoid pulling the paint off the wall when you remove a site-built countertop, score the caulking along the top edge of the backsplash with a utility knife. Cut any caulk or glue in the joint between the cabinet frame and the countertop. Keep the blade perpendicular to the frame to avoid cutting the wood. Pry the countertop off the frame with a pry bar.

5 If the countertop is too heavy even with the sink removed, you can cut it into sections with a reciprocating saw. Protect the cabinets if you plan to reuse them and make the first cut in the front edge of the sink cutout. You may have to work from below the countertop to cut the rear section and backsplash.

refrigerator out of the way will make prying easier.

Before removing the sink, shut the water off. If your faucets have stop valves on the supply lines, turn the water off at the valves. If valves are not present, turn the water off at the main supply valve. Install shut-off valves before you put in your new countertop. (See "Ortho's All About Plumbing Basics.")

The sink trap will always contain a small amount of water, so set a bucket under the trap to catch any spills. Loosen the compression nuts that fasten the various pieces of the trap assembly and pull the trap apart. Then stuff a rag into the extension tube in the wall to keep vent gases from entering the room.

Old countertops that were originally installed on-site may be nailed and glued to the top of the cabinet frame. Cut any glue line as completely as possible before you try to pry them off. If a utility knife won't score deeply enough, insert a thin putty knife in the joint and work it back and forth to cut the glue. You may damage the cabinets when removing this type of top.

REMOVING A SINK

Most kitchen and bathroom sinks are mounted in one of three ways, shown at right. No matter what kind of sink you have, remove it before you take off the countertop.

■ First, disconnect all water supply lines, traps, and dishwasher drain lines from the sink and garbage disposal unit.

■ Loosen and remove the retaining ring screws on the garbage disposal and rotate the disposal clockwise to drop it away from the sink.

■ Score any caulking around the edge of the sink and loosen any retaining screws or clips.

■ Insert a pry bar under the edge of the sink and pry it up until you can grip it with your hands. Be careful not to chip porcelain or enameled cast-iron sinks.

■ Lift the sink up and out of the countertop. A cast-iron sink can weigh 100 pounds or more, so ask for help with one. Save the hardware if you will reinstall the sink.

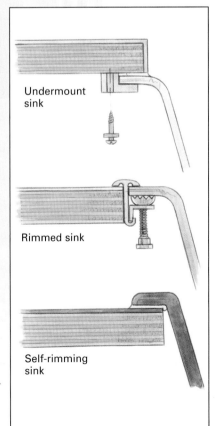

Undermount
sink

Rimmed sink

Self-rimming
sink

REMOVING OLD CABINETS

Removing cabinets is not a difficult job, but it can be messy and time consuming. Protect your floors and any other surfaces such as tables, work areas, computer equipment, or entertainment centers by either removing them or covering them with heavy kraft paper or old rugs. To keep dust from migrating into other areas of the house, keep entrances to your work area closed or tape clear polyethylene sheets to the jambs to seal them. Put an old rug down at the doorways to minimize the amount of dust you track out of the work area.

REUSE YOUR OLD CABINETRY

Modular cabinets can be removed and reused in the basement, utility room, or—if in good condition—even in renovated family rooms. You may be able to find similar uses for old metal cabinets. They may be unsuitable for kitchen or bath use, but spruced up with a coat of paint, they can make a great addition to your garage storage. Save the old doors and drawers and fit them to other storage areas that you've built yourself. Even if you have no further use for your existing cabinets, a local charitable organization may find a use for

them if they are sound and their surfaces are in good condition. And if you plan to reuse the hardware, clean the pieces and store them along with mounting hardware in plastic bags.

HOW CABINETS ARE ATTACHED

Depending on their age and method of manufacture, cabinets are attached to walls in a variety of ways. You may find yours nailed or screwed into the studs behind the surface of the walls. Some upper units may be fastened to the soffit. Base units may be nailed into the floor. Metal cabinets are usually hung on brackets screwed to the studs. Before you start dismantling, study the cabinets to determine how they were installed so you will know how to make removal easier.

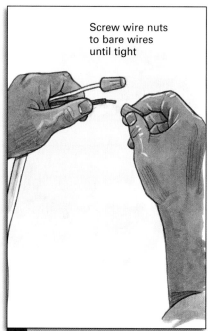

1 At the main service panel, turn off the power to any circuits feeding undercabinet lighting or vent hoods. Disconnect the wires and remove the fixture. Protect bare wires from shorting with wire nuts.

Screw wire nuts to bare wires until tight

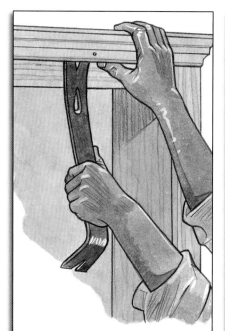

2 Insert a pry bar under moldings and remove them in sections. If you intend to reuse the moldings, pry as close to each nail as possible to avoid splitting the wood. If you can't get a pry bar under the molding, insert a wide putty knife.

Valance

Face frame stile

3 Remove the valances— the decorative pieces that fit between the cabinets where there are windows. If the valances are screwed to the face frames, remove the screws. Pry or cut nailed valances from the stiles.

DISMANTLING IN ORDER

No matter how your cabinetry is installed, follow these steps to save time.

■ Remove appliances first. Disconnect sink plumbing and remove the sink.

■ Remove the countertop (see page 38).

■ Take out the drawers and remove the doors. This will make it easier for you to see into the units so you can determine how and where they are fastened.

■ In most cases, removing the lower units first will be easiest and will allow you to get under the top units more easily.

■ Unscrew the fasteners or pry nailed units from the wall. To remove metal cabinets, loosen the hanger screws, lift the cabinets off the hangers, and remove the screws.

■ New cabinets are seldom the same sizes as the old, so expect to repair some spots on the walls and repaint them. Keep wall damage to a minimum and patch and smooth damaged areas before repainting.

■ If your room will have ceramic tile or wood floors, lay the floor before installing your new cabinets. Install vinyl flooring or carpet after the new cabinets are in place.

REMOVING APPLIANCES

Removing appliances before you begin dismantling cabinets will make the job easier. Once you have disconnected large appliances, use an appliance dolly to move them out of the work area.

■ **DROP-IN RANGES.** Unplug the unit or shut off the gas supply valve and disconnect the gas flex line. Lift the unit up and out of the countertop.

■ **VENTILATED COOKTOPS.** Disconnect the venting system under the countertop. Unplug the range or shut off the gas and disconnect the flex line. Lift the unit out.

■ **FREESTANDING STOVE.** Pull the unit out slightly from the wall and unplug it or shut off the gas supply valve and disconnect the gas flex line. Take the stove to another room or move it out of the way.

■ **WALL OVENS.** Unplug the unit or shut off the gas valve (it's usually under the oven). Remove fasteners holding the flange to the cabinet frame. Lift the unit out.

If an electric appliance is wired directly to the circuit, turn the power off and put tape over the circuit breaker to alert other members of the household not to turn it on. Disconnect the appliance in the junction box and cap the wires in the box with wire nuts. Don't turn the power back on until an electrician inspects the junction box.

■ **DISHWASHER.** Shut off the water supply valve and disconnect the dishwasher drain hose. Unscrew the unit from the face frame at the flanges. Pull the dishwasher out from under the countertop.

■ **TRASH COMPACTOR.** Remove the screws through the flanges. Pull the unit out and unplug it.

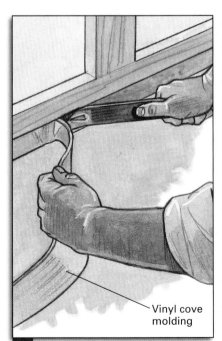

4 Using a pry bar or a wide putty knife, peel vinyl cove molding from the toe-kicks. If the toe-kicks are trimmed with quarter-round or other wooden base molding, pry up the molding with a pry bar. Number the pieces if you plan to reuse them.

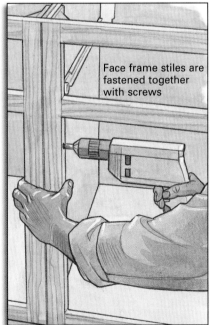

Face frame stiles are fastened together with screws

5 Take out all the drawers and remove the doors. Then separate the face frames that are fastened together by unscrewing the fasteners with a drill/driver. If the face frames are nailed, cut them apart with a reciprocating saw.

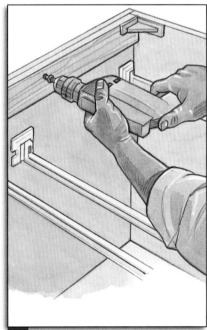

6 Most cabinets are fastened to the wall with screws or nails driven through the back. Remove screws or pry nailed cabinetry from the wall with a pry bar. Insert a wide piece of scrap under the bar to avoid damaging the wall.

Painting cabinets adds more than new color. Choosing the right color and changing the hardware can alter the style so dramatically that your guests might think the cabinets are new. Choose quality paints and brushes—they will give you a professional-looking finish.

Routing rabbets in doors will let you replace flat or raised panels with glass panes, adding visual depth to your cabinets and brightening the room. Clear glass will show off the cabinet contents, or you can order stained-glass inserts or frosted glass to hide things.

Wood veneer has to be aligned precisely. Cutting it slightly oversize for each member of the face frame will allow you to adjust its placement before adhering it to the surface.

When you replace doors, you should replace the drawer fronts, too. Make sure the drawers are properly aligned before you fasten them.

FACELIFTS

Sometimes a simple facelift can work wonders on your existing cabinets. Painting or refinishing can give drab slab-door designs a contemporary, modern look or freshen a tired country design. Stenciling and other decorative painting techniques can give your existing cabinets new style and personality, turning ordinary cabinets into unique decorator items. Installing new doors and drawer fronts and refacing the cabinets with veneers or laminates will update those cabinets that were in style decades ago. A facelift will bring your kitchen or bath—or a cabinet in any room—up-to-date at a cost far below the price of new cabinetry.

Altering the appearance of the skin of the cabinets is the best form of recycling, but it can be labor intensive. With the exception of simple door replacements, all of the facelift techniques require at least a weekend of work, and usually more.

Careful planning—even for such seemingly simple tasks as repainting—will help make the job go smoothly and give you professional-looking results. And as in any redecorating task, you should precede the actual work with some thorough research into style and material options.

No matter what method you choose to change the appearance of your cabinets, consider the cost of materials as an investment, not an expense. Buy the highest-quality paint, stain, varnish, doors, and refacing materials you can afford. They will reward you with additional years of usefulness and reduced maintenance requirements.

SAFETY HAZARDS

Changing the face of cabinets is less likely to cause physical injury than other remodeling activities. Always use the same standard safety equipment as you would for other tasks—gloves, and ear and eye protection.

Working with paints, solvents, strippers, stains, and other finishes demands extra protection. Many of these materials are caustic and harmful if breathed. Wear a respirator and keep windows open to provide adequate ventilation. Rubber gloves are a must when handling strippers and solvents. Wear them even with paints and stains that are not particularly dangerous—they will keep your hands clean.

INSTALLING CROWN MOLDING

Adding crown molding to your cabinets is a great finishing touch. Installing it may require a nailer on the molding to attach the molding to the cabinets. Glue 1× stock to the back of the molding pieces, then measure the first side piece from the factory edge and cut it at a 45-degree angle. Use a miter saw for accurate cuts, clamping the piece securely against the fence. Install one piece before measuring the other.

Attach the molding from the rear of the cabinet if possible, using No. 8 screws long enough to penetrate the nailer but not so long they will poke through its face. Hold the piece in place and predrill the holes to avoid splitting the stock.

PAINTING CABINETS

Painting your cabinets, whether they are in a kitchen, rec room, bath, or children's playroom, is the quickest and least expensive way to give them a facelift.

PREPARING FOR THE PAINT

Preparation is the key to a smooth paint job. Begin preparation by washing and sanding the surfaces. Washing removes grease and grime that make sanding, or deglossing, impossible. Sanding gives the old finish tooth—a slightly roughened surface that improves the adhesion of the new paint. Sand with the grain until the shine on the surface becomes dull. Don't sand so deeply you go through to bare wood. Scrape off loose finish.

Before painting, fill depressions and spots left bare from scraping with latex filler, then sand smooth. Fill and sand hardware holes if you are changing pulls or hinges.

A complete paint job usually requires a coat of primer and two coats of the finish paint. Check the paint manufacturer's specifications to see whether a primer is required (it is needed over a urethane finish). If priming unfinished cabinetry with a latex primer, sand the dried primer lightly with 220-grit sandpaper. And whatever paint you use, buy the highest quality you can afford.

PAINTING TIPS

Before you start painting, dip the brush up to its ferrule in water (for latex paints) or paint thinner (for oil-base paints) and tap out the excess liquid. This will keep the paint from drying up at the ferrule and stiffening.

Then, after dipping the brush in about an inch of paint, cut the paint in at the edges of the surface, working from unpainted to painted areas.

Paint wide surfaces with a short-nap (¼-inch) roller. The roller will leave a slight pattern, which you must lay off (brush out) with a brush. While the surface is wet, pull the tip of the brush through the paint in long, overlapping strokes.

Finish up by working the brush with the grain from one end of the surface to the other. The interior of the cabinets is a great place to practice this procedure. Don't worry about the small brush marks left in the paint. They will level themselves out as the paint dries. When the first coat has dried, apply the second coat using the same techniques.

To keep a brush fresh during breaks, suspend it in solvent (water for latex paint). Keep rollers pliable in airtight bags.

When cleaning a brush, shake it back and forth in a one-gallon container of water or paint thinner. Spin it out with a spinner and repeat the process with fresh thinner. Dispose of thinning liquids in the proper manner.

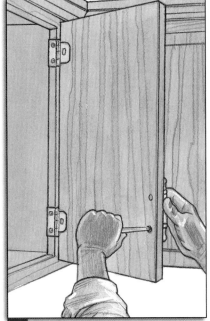

Sand recesses with flexible sanding block or bend sandpaper around a large dowel

1 *Empty the cabinets and the drawers, then pull the drawers off their slides and take off the doors at their hinges. Remove all hinges, pulls, knobs, and closers, and store them if you plan to reuse them.*

2 *Wash all cabinet surfaces, doors, and drawer fronts with a mild solution of trisodium phosphate. When dry, remove loose or peeling paint with a scraper and sand the surfaces lightly with 120–150-grit sandpaper. Wipe off with a tack rag.*

TOOLBOX

■ Phillips and flathead screwdrivers or cordless drill
■ Wide and narrow putty knives
■ Random-orbit sander, coarse and fine grits
■ Masking tape
■ 2½-inch brush
■ Paint tray and liners
■ Roller handle and two or three lamb's wool sleeves
■ Primer and paint
■ Thinner for oil-base paints
■ Tack cloth

PAINTS AND BRUSHES

Cabinets—especially those in kitchens, baths, and children's playrooms—need a hard surface that will stand up to wear and repeated cleanings.

The hardest paint surface for home use, modified alkyd paint, comes in aerosol spray cans. Spray painting, even with aerosol cans, is an art. Sprayed improperly, paint will sag and run. If you use this method, protect surfaces you don't want painted by masking them off well beyond the painted areas.

Alkyd or oil-base paints are tough, durable, high-gloss paints. They dry quickly, some within 48 hours, which is an advantage if you have to use the cabinets in a short period of time. These paints have a strong oil smell and require thinner for cleanup. An oil-base primer is required when painting over a urethane finish. Latex paints won't stick to urethane.

Acrylic water-base paints are the easiest to apply and produce an acceptable gloss and hardness. They take longer to cure, however; some as long as a week. Cleanup with water is easier than with oil paints.

Use natural-bristle brushes with oil paints, synthetic bristles for latex paints.

PAINT BY THE NUMBERS

Spraying is the easiest way to paint cabinets and doors. However, spraying puts paint not only on the cabinets, but also on surfaces you don't want painted. You can rent spraying equipment. Spraying is an effective way to paint new, unfinished cabinets that you can finish off-site before installing. Spray painting is impractical for existing cabinets, though.

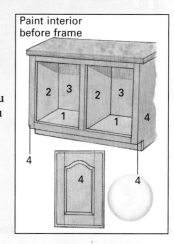
Paint interior before frame

When painting cabinet face frames and other surfaces with grain running in different planes, paint the shortest members first. Painting in the order shown above allows you to finish the brushstrokes off the piece. That way, the horizontal brushstrokes from painting parts 2 and 3 will be painted out when the brush passes over the stiles (4).

Cut in edges first with narrow brush

3 Paint cabinet interiors first, starting at the top of the cabinets and working down. Use a brush for narrow surfaces and to cut in at the edges. Then use a wide brush or short-nap roller. Follow the same procedure on the exterior.

2× scrap raises door off tarp to allow edge painting

4 Cover a horizontal work surface with plastic tarps or newspaper. Support the doors with 2× scrap so you can paint the edges without dragging the brush on the work surface. When one side is dry, paint the other.

5 Stand drawers on their back ends and paint the drawer fronts. Leave the drawer box unpainted. Let the paint dry thoroughly before reinstalling the hardware.

STRIPPING AND REFINISHING

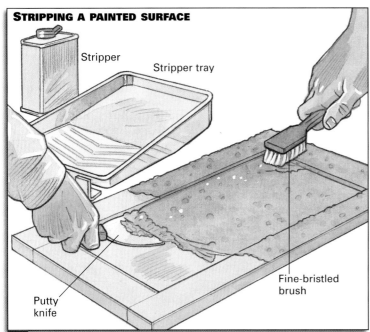

STRIPPING A PAINTED SURFACE

Stripper

Stripper tray

Fine-bristled brush

Putty knife

1 Brush on stripper and let it set until the paint begins to bubble along its entire surface. Then scrape off the loosened paint with a paint scraper or wide putty knife, taking care not to gouge the wood. Use a fine-bristled brush or steel wool to remove the paint from recessed surfaces. Reapply stripper and repeat the process as necessary. Remove stripper residue with mineral spirits or the solvent recommended by the manufacturer.

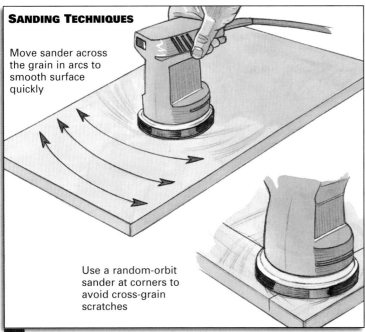

SANDING TECHNIQUES

Move sander across the grain in arcs to smooth surface quickly

Use a random-orbit sander at corners to avoid cross-grain scratches

2 Start with a medium grit and work up to finer grits, using aluminum oxide paper. Sand slowly to avoid sanding through veneered surfaces. Check the surface frequently with your fingertips to make sure it is uniformly smooth. When the sanding is complete, vacuum the cabinets to remove excess dust and wipe all surfaces with a tack cloth.

Stripping and refinishing cabinets is an inexpensive but time-consuming task. It is, however, especially practical for limited budgets, on small spans of cabinetry, or when you want to darken the look of cabinets that you are otherwise satisfied with. It's also the perfect way to integrate antique furniture into your current design.

PREPARATION STEPS

Any flaws in the piece will be magnified by the final finish, so take care of them before you start.

Gently slide a putty knife under the edges of loose veneer and squeeze glue into the recess. Hardware stores sell squeeze bottles with narrow metal spouts made especially for getting glue into tight spots. Clamp the repair, using waxed paper between the clamp and the wood. The waxed paper prevents glue seepage from sticking to the clamp. Leave dings and depressions until you have stripped the surface, then level them with filler that matches the final finish.

STRIPPING TIPS

Read the label for specific directions for using the stripper. Protect your floor with a plastic

TOOLBOX

- Brushes or applicators for stripper, stain, and finishes
- 3-inch putty knife or scraper
- Steel wool or nylon abrasive pads
- Small fine-bristled wire brushes
- Sandpaper, various grits
- Finishing or random-orbit sander
- Clean containers for solvents, stains, and finishes
- Filler and burlap
- Rags

SANDPAPER AND GRITS

For rough sanding, use sandpaper in the 80- to 100-grit range. Switch to a medium paper with 150 or 180 grit, and finish with 220-grit paper.

Sanding does not need to proceed through every grit. You can start with 80-grit paper, skip to a 120-grit paper, and go from there to a 220-grit abrasive. Make sure the marks left by the previous grit are removed before using the next one.

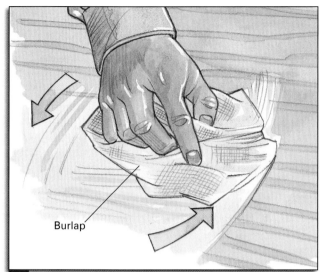

Burlap

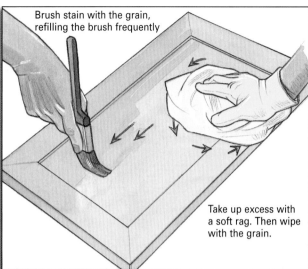

Brush stain with the grain, refilling the brush frequently

Take up excess with a soft rag. Then wipe with the grain.

3 *Thin the filler according to the instructions on the label and color it with pigments if necessary. Apply the filler with a piece of burlap (available at crafts stores), using a circular motion and moderate pressure to force the filler into the grain. When the entire surface is covered, wipe it lightly in the direction of the grain. Allow it to dry for 24 hours.*

4 *Use natural bristles for oil- or solvent-base stains, synthetic bristles for water-base stains. Apply the stain with a 3-inch brush, loading the brush frequently and applying it to the surface in the direction of the grain. Let the stain set according to the time specified by the manufacturer and wipe up the excess with a soft, clean cloth. Let dry and seal if required for the finish.*

tarp covered with newspaper. Working from the top down, apply the stripper with a brush; don't brush it out of the wood. Round the corners of a 3-inch putty knife to minimize gouges in the wood. When using steel wool, start with 00, then use 000 and 0000.

PASTE AND LIQUID STRIPPERS

Paste strippers are thick and cling to vertical surfaces, making stripping cabinetry more manageable. They are also more powerful than liquid strippers. Liquid strippers work well on thin finishes applied to horizontal surfaces or in removing residues left by paste strippers. Furniture restorers are weak strippers that allow you to remove thin finishes without leaving gouges.

10–12" from surface

Finish spray stroke here and start the next stroke with an overlap of about 2 inches

Start spray stroke here

Can held parallel to surface

Brushing on

Tipping off

Hold the can parallel to the surface and about 10 to 12 inches away from it. Start spraying slightly beyond the edge of the surface and move across it. Release the spray valve slightly beyond the opposite edge. Continue spraying in a back-and-forth motion, overlapping each stroke slightly.

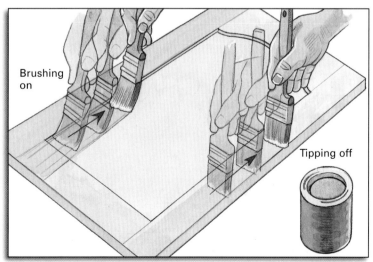

Apply varnish with a 3-inch brush, working in long strokes with the grain and with even pressure. When the surface is completely covered, tip it off to level it, using only the tip of the brush held almost perpendicular to the surface. If the varnish bubbles, thin it by 10 percent with the solvent recommended by the manufacturer.

SPECIAL-EFFECT FINISHES

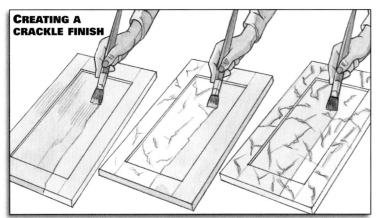

CREATING A CRACKLE FINISH

Paint one coat of the base color and let it dry completely. Depending on your design, paint the crackle medium on either the entire surface or portions of it. Let this coat dry thoroughly also. Apply the second coat of different-colored paint and let the crackling dry. Protect the surface with two coats of spray varnish.

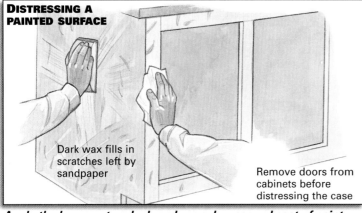

DISTRESSING A PAINTED SURFACE

Dark wax fills in scratches left by sandpaper

Remove doors from cabinets before distressing the case

Apply the base coat and when dry, apply a second coat of paint or a wax/pigment mixture. Let this coat dry, then scuff it with sandpaper using varied pressure until the base coat shows through. If using a wax/pigment mixture, polish it with a soft cloth and distress the wax sparingly. Rub with dark wax for an aged patina effect.

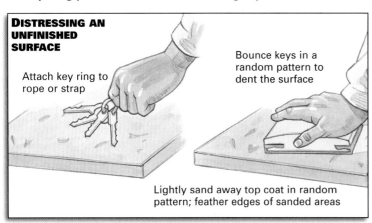

DISTRESSING AN UNFINISHED SURFACE

Attach key ring to rope or strap

Bounce keys in a random pattern to dent the surface

Lightly sand away top coat in random pattern; feather edges of sanded areas

Distress the unfinished surface or apply base coat and distress it in a random pattern with a combination of old keys—both large and small—fastened to a key ring. Bounce the keys randomly across the surface. Apply a second coat of contrasting paint and distress the finish using the techniques shown above.

TOOLBOX

- Paintbrushes, various sizes appropriate to the workpiece, natural bristle for oil paints, synthetic bristle for latex paints
- Sandpaper, 80, 120, 180 grits
- Palm sander or sanding block
- Tack cloth

Special-effect finishes add a custom look to old cabinets at a fraction of the cost of new cabinets.

Many special-effect techniques rely on the application of two coats of paint—a base coat of one color and a second coat of a contrasting color. Sanding the second coat lightly or splotching it when wet with plastic wrap, sponges, or rags lets the base coat show through in random areas, achieving an aged and used look. The crackle technique shown at top left simulates old paint that has cracked and peeled. The technique relies on a latex-vinyl second coat that separates when applied over a crackle emulsion.

UNFINISHED SURFACES

If you are using any of these techniques on unfinished surfaces, be sure to sand them smooth and fill dents or scratches before starting. Paint will not hide milling marks or other imperfections—it will only magnify them. Start with 80-grit sandpaper and proceed through 120-grit to 180-grit finish sanding. Round the corners of the workpieces slightly to enhance the look that they have been used. This will also help the paint adhere.

On unfinished cabinets, apply an oil-base stain-sealing primer coat under the base coat. The sealer keeps resins and oils in the wood from bleeding through the paint. Latex primers may work on individual pieces, but they tend to let resins around knots bleed through and mar the final finish.

CHOOSING COLORS

Your choice of colors can be as wide ranging as your imagination. Colors of the same hue—a dark green over a lighter green, for example—produce a classic look. Paint the first coat; if it looks rich and the primer doesn't show through, you may not need a second base coat. Otherwise, scuff it lightly with fine sandpaper or 000 steel wool, pick up the dust with a tack rag, apply another color coat, and let dry.

GLASS DOOR PANELS

Glass panes in doors can change the look of your cabinetry, adding visual depth and allowing the display of attractive kitchen utensils, dinnerware, or curios. Best of all, you can complete this modification easily in a weekend at very little cost.

Replacing wood with glass in a panel door requires routing out the rear edge of the dado (groove) that holds the panel in the door frame, removing the panel, and replacing it with glass. If you don't own a router, you can rent one. Tell the rental agent what you are doing so your router will be equipped with the proper straight bit for the job.

Remove the doors from the cabinet frame by unscrewing the hinges from the doors. Leave the hinges attached to the frame for easy replacement.

cushioning. Both of these styles may contain small staples or brads to keep the panels from rattling. Remove the fasteners before routing. If you can't get a grip on them, dig out the wood on the lip with a utility knife until you can grip them with a needle-nosed pliers. The router will remove the damaged spots.

When ordering the glass, specify dimensions $\frac{1}{16}$ to $\frac{1}{8}$ inch less than the actual opening. Although you may be tempted to order the glass after removing the first panel, wait until you have removed all of them. Then measure each. Opening sizes may vary; if they do, order glass sized for each door.

TOOLBOX

- ■ Screwdriver
- ■ Clear silicone caulk
- ■ Router

PREPARATION

In inset door construction, the edges of the door are assembled around the wood panel. With one exception—plywood panels— once you rout out the rear lip of the dado, you can remove the wood panel. Plywood panels are usually glued in place. Even after routing, you may find it difficult to pop the glued panel out without damaging the door.

Some doors have loose panels with edges cushioned by a piece of sponge rubber to allow for expansion and contraction. Other doors have floating panels with no

STAINED-GLASS APPLIQUÉ

You can turn your existing plain-pane cabinet doors into expensive-looking accents with a stained-glass appliqué kit. It uses translucent colorant that adheres to the glass and simulates the stained-glass look.

The kit comes with several patterns whose elements can be combined to suit your creativity. Application is simple— create the pattern, add lead beading on the glass, and color in the areas of the pattern.

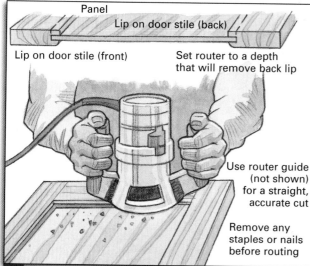

Panel
Lip on door stile (back)
Lip on door stile (front)
Set router to a depth that will remove back lip
Use router guide (not shown) for a straight, accurate cut
Remove any staples or nails before routing

1 *Working from the rear of the door, set the router to the depth of the inset panel and rout out the lip on the rear of the door. Drop the wood panel out of the door. Measure the length and width of the panel recess and order glass to fit.*

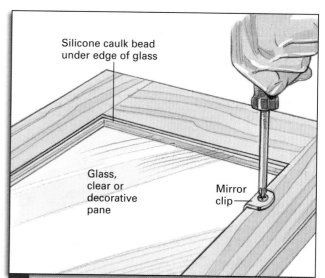

Silicone caulk bead under edge of glass
Glass, clear or decorative pane
Mirror clip

2 *Run a bead of clear silicone caulk on the lip of the panel recess and set the glass in place. The caulk will help eliminate rattling. Predrill holes in the door stiles and rails at 8-inch intervals and screw mirror clips to hold the glass in place.*

REFACING WITH VENEERS AND LAMINATES

Glued-on wood veneer or plastic laminate facings will make old cabinets look like new ones.

WOOD VENEER

Wood veneer applies in strips. Installation requires that you cut each veneer piece individually to fit the section of the frame on which you will apply it. There are three techniques for strip laminating:

■ Veneer the front faces only and leave the interior edges uncovered. This method is the fastest and least expensive, but when the cabinet doors are open, the uncovered edges show clearly you've refaced the frames.

■ Veneer the faces and edges separately. This method covers all visible surfaces and will make your existing cabinets look new. However, measuring and cutting each edge separately is time consuming, and the butted corner is easily damaged.

■ Veneer the face frame with wide strips and wrap them to cover the edges. This method calls for a thin 10-mil veneer to make the bend on the edges. It requires less work than cutting face and edge pieces separately and results in professional-looking edges that are not as vulnerable to damage.

This section shows the wrapped-edge technique. If you choose either of the other two methods, cut and trim the pieces individually and disregard the instructions for wrapping the edges.

PLASTIC LAMINATE

You can install plastic laminate using the strip method or sheet method.

TOOLBOX

FOR WOOD VENEER
■ Screwdrivers or cordless drill
■ Wide putty knife
■ Clamps
■ Small wood plane
■ Sanding tools and sandpaper
■ Woodworking glue
■ Utility knife
■ Hammer or brad nailer
■ Router
■ Brushes
■ Veneering tool or metal or wood roller
■ Trisodium phosphate (TSP)

**FOR PLASTIC LAMINATE
(IN ADDITION TO ABOVE)**
■ Carbide scoring tool or hand slitter
■ Laminate trimmer
■ File

1 *Remove the hinges from both the doors and cabinet frames. Store the hinges and screws if you plan to reuse them. Take out the drawers and remove the slides if they extend to a surface that will be refaced. Using a thin putty knife, pry up and remove moldings.*

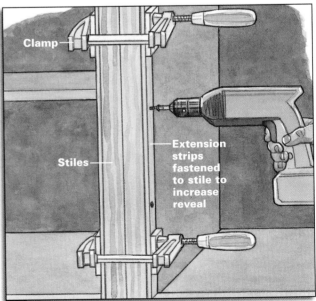

Clamp

Stiles

Extension strips fastened to stile to increase reveal

2 *Make sure the stiles are tightly fastened to each other. If you can move them by pulling on them, drive screws into predrilled holes. If your new doors require wider stiles, clamp extensions and glue and screw them into place. Clean the cabinets with TSP.*

Block plane removes uneven stile edges and levels stile surfaces

Construction adhesive

3 Plane all meeting surfaces to ensure that your refacing material will bond to them securely. Remove loose or peeling finishes and fill flaked areas and depressions with filler. Sand these areas smooth and scuff-sand the entire cabinet to ensure a good bond.

4 Measure and cut plywood panels slightly oversize for the bottom, and install them with construction adhesive and brads. Tape will hold the panel in place while driving the brads.

■ The strip method is less expensive—you cover only the outer faces with plastic and paint the inside edges (plastic laminate is too thick to allow scoring and bending around the edges of the frame).

■ The sheet method involves covering the entire face frame with one sheet of laminate, then routing out the door and drawer openings. It is more costly because of the amount of waste material, but requires very little cutting. Your refacing job will go twice as fast with the sheet method.

To strip-laminate your cabinets, follow the instructions on these pages, disregarding the information about wrapping the edges. Sheet laminating steps are shown on page 55.

GENERAL PREPARATION TIPS

Refacing with either wood veneer or plastic requires clean, smooth surfaces that are flush at their joints. Here is a summary of the steps needed to ready your cabinets and to make the job go smoothly.

■ Bring your refacing materials into the work area several days before you plan to install them. This will allow the materials to become acclimated to the temperature and humidity of the room.

■ When taking out drawers that you will reuse, number them so that any slight variations won't cause misfits.

■ Remove moldings with a wide putty knife. Pry the moldings off at each nail so you don't split the wood.

■ Make sure the cabinet frame is securely attached to the wall. Drive new screws into the studs if necessary.

■ Wash the entire surface with a mild solution of trisodium phosphate (TSP). Don't soak the surfaces, just scrub them enough to remove the grease and grime.

■ If your new doors are narrower than the old ones, fasten extensions into the openings. Extensions should be wide enough to allow the doors to overlap the openings by at least $\frac{3}{8}$ inch. Rip the strips from 1× stock and attach them with woodworking adhesive and brads. Fill the gap between the extension and the frame when you apply the finish.

■ Check adjoining face frames with a straightedge to ensure they are flush with one another. If they are not, clamp them with moderate pressure and tap them flush with a hammer, then tighten the clamps securely. Secure them with No. 6 drywall screws that penetrate into the second stile by at least half its width. Predrill the screw holes.

■ Examine the joints between the rails and stiles and fill them if they are not flush. When filling these joints or other imperfections—dents, dings, depressions, and flaked paint—use a latex filler or auto-body repair compound. Then sand the filler smooth with a palm sander or sanding block. After sanding, pick up the dust with a tack rag.

■ See if the side rails stand proud of the cabinet sides. If they do, you can cover the sides with ¼-inch plywood or rout or plane the rails flush with the cabinet sides.

REFACING WITH VENEERS AND LAMINATES
continued

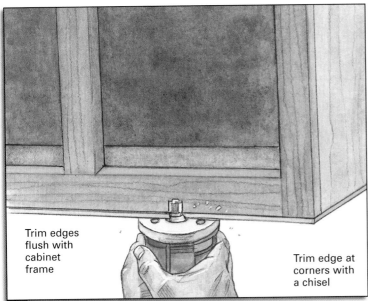

Trim edges flush with cabinet frame

Trim edge at corners with a chisel

5 *Using a router and a guided bit, trim the excess from the bottom panel so that it's flush with the cabinet face frame. Fill all the exposed edges of plywood with filler and sand them smooth. Filling them ensures a smooth surface for a good bond.*

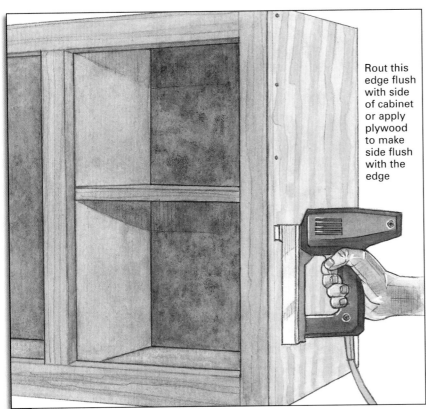

Rout this edge flush with side of cabinet or apply plywood to make side flush with the edge

6 *If the stiles extend beyond the cabinet sides, you can either rout them flush with the sides or fill the recess with a plywood panel. Cut the length of the panel slightly oversize and fasten it with construction adhesive and brads. Trim the excess flush with the cabinet frame with a utility knife or laminate trimmer.*

APPLYING WOOD VENEER

Applying wood veneer requires a few special techniques:

■ **IMPROVING THE BOND:** Although the pressure-sensitive adhesive on most veneers will stick reasonably well, it should never be applied to unfinished wood because over time it will gradually peel off. Even over finished surfaces that have been cleaned and scuff-sanded, the bond can give way and the veneer will tend to delaminate.

You can improve the bond of the veneer over any surface and virtually guarantee its longevity by sealing the surface with lacquer, varnish, or a water-base (not solvent-base) contact adhesive. Lacquer sprays on easily and dries quickly, but many coats are required to seal the pores of unfinished wood. Lacquer may also lift certain varnishes and paints off previously finished cabinets.

Varnish application is easy with a brush, but varnish can take a long time to cure.

Brushing on a thin coat of water-base contact adhesive takes little time. It dries in about 30 minutes.

Whatever product you use to seal your cabinets, apply it to the face frames in sections. For example, seal the stiles first, then laminate them before sealing the rails. Premeasure the veneer pieces, then cut them while the sealant cures.

■ **CUTTING WOOD VENEER:** Although tools are manufactured specifically for cutting wood veneer, an ordinary utility knife with a sharp blade does a great job. Before starting your project, invest in several packages of high-quality blades, and as your work proceeds, change the blades often so your cuts are made with a sharp edge. Resist the temptation to make a cut with a blade that's starting to dull. It takes only seconds to change blades and those seconds can save you time and money if you don't have to throw out a damaged piece of veneer.

Always cut wood veneer faceup, using a metal straightedge with a nonskid back as a guide. Hold the straightedge securely or clamp it to the work surface. When cutting the line with the blade, work slowly and make your first pass a light one. Cutting in several passes with increasing pressure will help the blade find its own path in the wood,

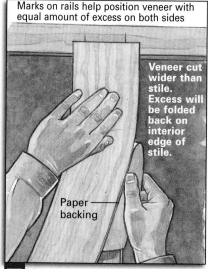

Marks on rails help position veneer with equal amount of excess on both sides

Veneer cut wider than stile. Excess will be folded back on interior edge of stile.

Paper backing

7 *Cut veneer for the center stiles wider and longer than the stile. Mark the stile position on the rails so you can center the veneer on the stile. Peel a little of the paper backing and stick the veneer lightly at the top. Peel the paper and press the veneer down as you go.*

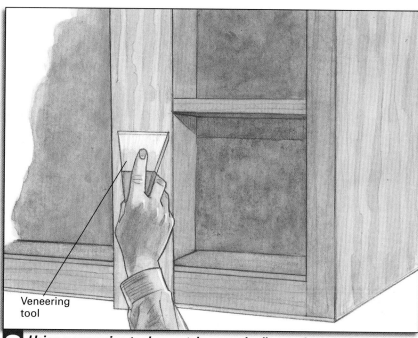

Veneering tool

8 *Using a veneering tool or metal or wood roller, apply pressure along the stile only, not to the excess edges of the veneer. Smoothing the veneer adheres it to the surface and removes small air bubbles.*

reducing the tendency to wander off with the grain pattern. Use the same technique when making cross-grain cuts. Cut clear through the paper backing. If you encounter a section with a knot or blemish, don't use it in a conspicuous place.

■ **ORGANIZE YOUR WORK:** Strip application proceeds in the following order— the bottom of the cabinet, the sides, the vertical face pieces (the stiles), and finally,

the horizontal face sections (the rails). Cut long pieces first, then shorter ones.

■ **VENEERING THE STILES:** Cut the width and then the length, making both dimensions about ½ inch wider and longer than the

WHAT IF I MAKE A MISTAKE?

Refacing cabinets with wood veneer or plastic laminate requires precision. Sooner or later, you're bound to apply a piece that's crooked or too short. If you do, remove it immediately. You'll find that removal is difficult, but not impossible if you act quickly. The adhesive doesn't cure to its full strength for several days.

First remove the veneer by scraping and pulling at the same time. Often the surface will come up, leaving an adhesive residue. Soften the adhesive with mineral spirits and scrape it off completely. If mineral spirits don't work, try spray penetrating oil. Repair any damage to the surface before you set the new piece in place.

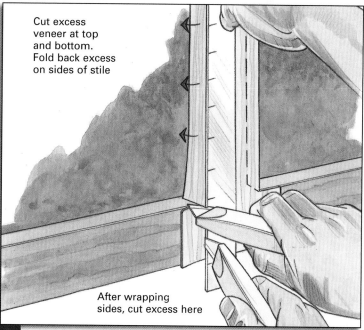

Cut excess veneer at top and bottom. Fold back excess on sides of stile

After wrapping sides, cut excess here

9 *Using a utility knife, cut the top and bottom of the veneer at the edge of the rails. Start the point of the knife on the edge of the veneer and slice up to the stile. Fold back the edges of the veneer and press them to the stile. Then cut off the excess veneer at the top and bottom rails using a straightedge as a guide.*

REFACING WITH VENEERS AND LAMINATES
continued

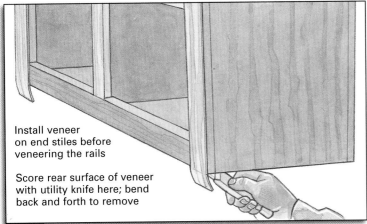

Install veneer on end stiles before veneering the rails

Score rear surface of veneer with utility knife here; bend back and forth to remove

10 *Using the techniques above, cut and install veneer on the end stiles, folding it back on the interior edges. Trim the top and bottom excess by scoring the back of the veneer at the cabinet frame and bending it until it breaks.*

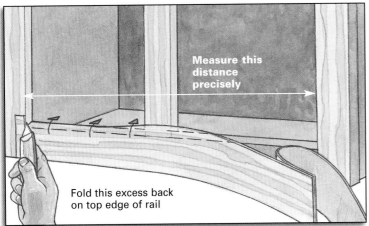

Measure this distance precisely

Fold this excess back on top edge of rail

11 *Cut a veneer strip wider than the rail by its thickness and 1 inch longer. Butt a squared end against the stile and nick the other end precisely where it falls on the veneer. Cut the strip to length and apply it to the the rail, folding back the top edge.*

12 *Using 100-grit sandpaper, lightly sand all the edges of the veneer, being careful not to cut through to the paper. If the veneer is prestained, touch up sanded edges with matching stain. Fill joints with finishing putty, sand smooth, and varnish.*

actual measurements. For example, if a stile is 2 inches wide and ¾ inch thick, your veneer should be 4 inches wide (2 inches for the stile, 1½ inches for the two edge wraparounds, and ½ inch excess). Don't bother cutting complex pieces where two stiles of different heights join. Cut the veneer to the total width required, including the excess. Then cut it to fit the configuration of the cabinets after you have applied it.

■ **BEFORE YOU VENEER THE STILES,** mark the top and bottom rails at points that will center the veneer piece. Then peel back about an inch of paper from the top of the veneer. Place the piece over the top rail with a slight overhang and align it with the marks. Tap the top lightly to adhere it, and holding the veneer in place with one hand, pull the paper off with the other, stopping frequently to tap it lightly as you go. Then smooth the piece with a laminate tool or roller.

■ **VENEERING THE RAILS:** Cover the cabinet rails the same way as the stiles—longer pieces first, then shorter ones, each about ½ inch wider than the rail width.

First stick tape to the veneered stiles and mark the location of the rail piece—usually at a point that brings the bottom of the rail veneer flush with the bottom of the rail. Then cut the rail veneer about an inch longer than required. Hold the piece squared to one stile joint and score the other end with a utility knife precisely where it meets the veneer on the opposite stile. Remove the piece and cut it to length. Recheck the fit and apply, peeling back the paper a little at a time. Fold the veneer back on the exposed edge of the rail.

■ **SAND THE EDGES LIGHTLY WITH 100-GRIT PAPER:** Touch up any prestained edges as required and apply the finish of your choice.

CUTTING PLASTIC LAMINATE

To cut plastic laminate, lay the sheet faceup on a flat surface and score the cut line with a carbide scoring tool. Use a metal straightedge as a guide. After scoring two or three times, lift up one side and the laminate will snap cleanly.

You can also cut laminate with a hand slitter (a slightly more expensive tool) or on a table saw equipped with a fine-toothed blade. When using a table saw, install a cutting guide to keep the laminate from sliding under the rip fence.

APPLYING PLASTIC LAMINATE

Plastic laminate is applied in essentially the same manner as strip laminating wood veneer. Because the corners don't wrap around, there are a few variations. Cut the pieces oversize.

■ **APPLY PLASTIC LAMINATE WITH CONTACT ADHESIVE:** This adhesive comes as a brush-on product or in aerosol spray cans. Spray adhesive is slightly more expensive, but you might find it easier to apply an even coat with it. The brush-on adhesive will probably work better on larger pieces. Apply adhesive to both the cabinet surface and the back of the laminate. Let the adhesive cure as specified on the material label. Position the laminate precisely before applying it. Contact adhesive grabs immediately, so your positioning has to be precise.

■ **AFTER ADHERING,** trim the excess with a laminate trimmer. You can also use a router, but the small size and light weight of the laminate trimmer give you more control.

■ **AS AN AID TO ADHERING THE BOTTOM PIECE,** tape spacers to the front and apply the laminate from one side to the other, removing the spacers as you go.

■ **FILE BUTTED LAMINATE EDGES WITH A LAMINATE FILE:** Sand others lightly with 100-grit paper.

SHEET LAMINATING WITH PLASTIC LAMINATE

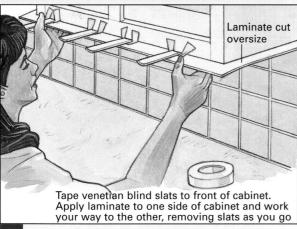

Laminate cut oversize

Tape venetian blind slats to front of cabinet. Apply laminate to one side of cabinet and work your way to the other, removing slats as you go

1 Fasten ¼-inch plywood to bottom and sides with construction adhesive and brads. Then cut laminate 1 inch larger than actual dimensions. Spray with contact adhesive and apply. Repeat for sides.

Sand edges smooth after trimming

2 Roll the surfaces with a wood or metal roller to remove any voids. Use a laminate trimmer to trim the excess from the edges. Then sand smooth with 100-grit sandpaper and a sanding block.

Contact adhesive applied to front of frame and back of sheet.

3 Cut the laminate 2 inches larger than the cabinet surface and apply contact adhesive to the face frame and laminate back. Position the laminate square to the frame, apply, smooth by hand, and roll.

Starter hole for laminate trimmer

4 Drill a starter hole and trim the laminate flush with the interior edges of the openings. Trim the exterior edges and roll all surfaces. File interior corners square and paint inside edges, if necessary.

REPLACING DOORS AND DRAWER FRONTS

The most critical aspect of replacing doors and drawer fronts is making them look right by centering them on their openings and keeping them square. Masking tape makes this task precise, but apply the tape lightly and pull it off gently to avoid pulling off the cabinet finish. If using a cordless drill to drive hinge screws, set its clutch to keep from overdriving the screws.

INSTALLING NEW DOORS

■ Apply 2-inch masking tape lightly along the entire run of the cabinets. Run the tape on the bottom of wall cabinets and the top of base cabinets. Using the reveals you noted on your layout sketch, mark the door positions on the masking tape—snap a chalk line along the entire run so all the doors will fall on the same line. Then mark the tape where you want the edges of the doors to fall.
■ Install hinges as shown below.
■ Hold the door on the marks and install one screw only in the top hinge plate. Leave the screw slightly loose and use it as a pivot to align the bottom of the door. Install the lower hinge with one screw, leaving it loose. Install the remaining doors in the same fashion.
■ Line up each door precisely and tighten the loose screws. Predrill and install the remaining screws on all doors. Remove the masking tape.

INSTALLING DRAWER FRONTS

■ Apply tape in the same way as for doors, and mark the tape for the exact placement of the drawer front.
■ Predrill the drawer box for the attachment screws. Insert the screws from the back of the drawer box and tighten them until just the point pokes through the front.
■ Insert the drawer box in the opening.
■ Holding the drawer front on the lines marked on the masking tape, reach behind the drawer and push it forward until the screw points indent the rear surface of the drawer front.
■ Remove the drawer and install the front, using the indented holes to position the screws. Do not overtighten the screws. Remove the masking tape gently.

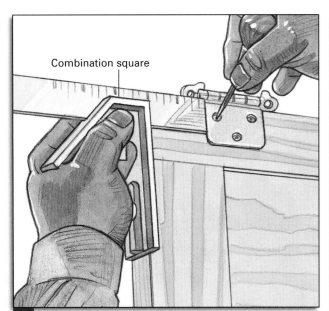

1 *Using a combination square, mark each door at 2 inches (or at a point that looks correct for the hinge) from both the top and bottom of the door. Set the hinge on your mark and mark the center of the holes. Predrill the holes and screw on the hinges.*

Combination square

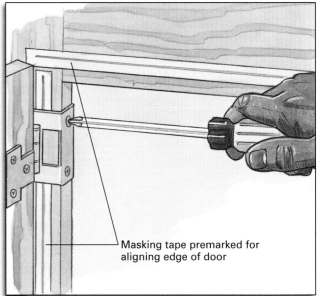

Masking tape premarked for aligning edge of door

2 *Put masking tape lightly along the length of the cabinet and on one side of each opening. Using the reveals from your layout drawing, mark the tape for the position of the door. Hold the door in place, mark the holes, and screw the plate down in predrilled holes.*

INSTALLING CUP HINGES

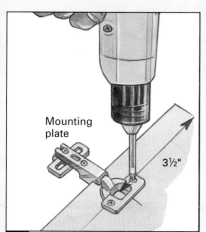

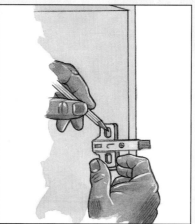

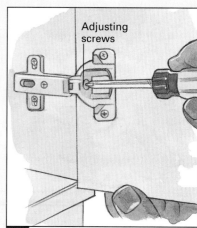

1 Drill the 35mm holes for the hinges, if necessary, spacing them 3½ inches to center from the top and bottom of the doors. Lay the door on a flat surface and set the hinge in the hole with the mounting plate attached. Align the hinge so it's perpendicular to the edge of the door and screw it into place.

2 Hold the door in place, centered on the opening, and mark the location of the mounting plates on the inside of the cabinet frame. Disassemble the mounting plates from the hinges and mark the location of the screws. Predrill the holes and fasten the mounting plates to the frame.

3 Insert both hinges in the mounting plates and tighten the adjustment screws slightly. Open and close the door and adjust its position, tightening the adjustment screws when the door is centered in its opening.

REPLACING DRAWER FRONTS

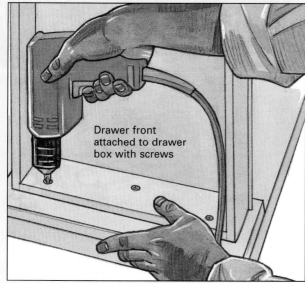

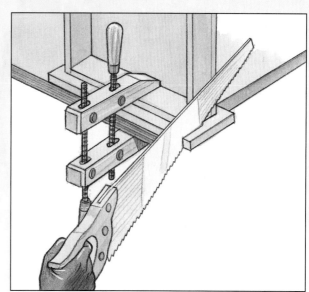

To replace the fronts on drawers with separate face panels, unscrew the fasteners that hold the front panel to the drawer box. Align the new panel with the drawer box and fasten it.

On drawers that have front panels integral to the drawer box, clamp the front panel and remove the edges with a handsaw. Align the box on the new panel and fasten it with screws of the proper length.

Installing new cabinets requires the same amount of organization as any other do-it-yourself task. Bring all the tools you need into the room so you don't have to dash to the garage or hardware store in the middle of the project. Hang wall cabinets first so you won't have to reach over the base cabinets. Make sure your new units are out of the way so they don't get damaged as you move the first ones into place.

INSTALLING NEW CABINETS

New cabinets enhance the appearance of any room in your house. They can also greatly increase the usefulness and convenience of any room. In the kitchen, new cabinets can turn what might have been a cramped and inefficient place to prepare meals into a bright, cheerful room. In the family room, they can house your entertainment equipment or books. New cabinetry can increase the efficiency of your home office, contributing to the bottom line of your home business or simply helping you to conduct household business with less stress and in less time.

Installing new cabinets yourself may seem formidable at first. But cabinet installation is simply a set of repetitive tasks, none of which requires more than basic skills and a few tools. And although the methods illustrated on the following pages pertain to kitchen cabinets, the same techniques apply to installations in any room.

SAFETY FIRST

Installing new cabinets is a relatively safe undertaking, but as with all remodeling projects, you should take steps to avoid injury.
■ Wear protection that is appropriate to the work at hand—eye protection and a respirator for any activity that produces dust, ear protection when using power tools, knee pads when working on the floor.
■ Avoid loose clothing that could get caught.
■ Always use the right tool for the job.
■ Work patiently and take a break when you get tired. More injuries happen when fatigue sets in.
■ When lifting, be careful to avoid back strain—bend your knees when lifting heavy materials such as wall cabinets. Enlist a helper whenever possible.

PREPARING THE ROOM FOR NEW CABINETS

Any homeowner with moderate skills and a few basic tools can install new cabinets relatively easily. Proper preparation of the room will get the job off to a good start and keep it moving smoothly.

CLEAR THE AREA

Clear the work area of all obstructions. You need sufficient working room to store and maneuver the cabinets. The less obstructed your work space is, the less likely you will damage the cabinets.

First remove all furniture and appliances either completely from the room or to a place in the work area that will keep them out of your way. Then remove all the old cabinets from the room.

PLAN THE FLOORING

If you're replacing the flooring with ceramic tile, set the cabinets on ¾-inch plywood cut to the dimensions of the base cabinets. That way you won't have problems refitting undercounter appliances into place. Lay wood flooring before installing the cabinets; other types of flooring can go in after the cabinets.

TOOLBOX

- Tape measure
- 4-foot level
- 6- to 8-foot 2×4
- Cordless drill
- Screwdriver tips
- Chalk line
- Stepladder
- Electronic stud finder

ADJUST FOR IMPERFECTIONS

Although your cabinets may be made perfectly square, it is unlikely you will find the same precision in the room. Floors are seldom level and walls are almost never perfect. Before you start, find the highest point on your floor as shown in illustration 1 below. Check wall surfaces for evenness using a 4-foot level.

CONSIDER THE COUNTERTOP

Measure up from the highest point on the floor to a height that will put your countertop at the level you have planned. Kitchen

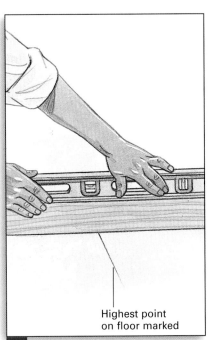

1 Using a long, straight 2×4 and a level, find the highest point on your floor. Mark the floor at this point. Fill in any large depressions in the wall with joint compound and sand smooth.

Highest point on floor marked

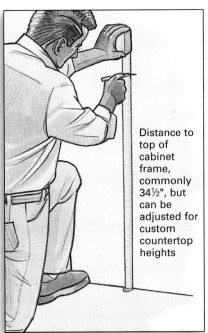

Distance to top of cabinet frame, commonly 34½", but can be adjusted for custom countertop heights

2 From the floor's high point, measure up 34½ inches (or to the height that when combined with the countertop thickness will put the countertop where you want it). Use a level to mark the wall along the entire length of the cabinetry.

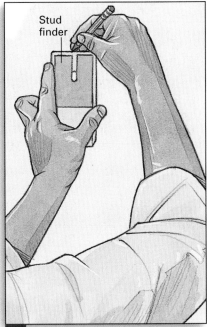

Stud finder

3 Use a stud finder to locate the studs in the wall. Mark the stud centers on the wall for both the upper cabinets and the base cabinets.

countertops are normally set at 36 inches above floor level. (See illustration 2 on the opposite page.) That 36-inch countertop height is not an absolute requirement, however. If your plans call for a different height, be sure to subtract the thickness of the countertop from your preferred height before marking the level line for the cabinet tops on the wall.

FIND THE STUDS

Cabinets must be fastened directly to the studs. You can find studs by tapping on the wall with a hammer and driving small nails, but using an electronic stud finder is easier and more accurate. This small, inexpensive device is sold at home centers and hardware stores. With it you can quickly find the exact centers of the studs.

NUMBER THE PIECES

To make cabinets lighter and easier to handle, remove the doors and drawers and store them in a safe place. This will protect them from damage too. Number the doors and drawers so you can put them back in their original places.

4 *Using a 4-foot carpenter's level, extend the cabinet reference line to all walls on which base cabinets will be installed. Make sure the line runs the full dimensions of all cabinet runs and is no less than the original height you measured.*

34½"

5 *Next, measure up 19½ inches from the base cabinet reference line. This mark represents the location of the bottom of the upper cabinets. Using a 4-foot level, extend this line to all walls on which upper cabinets will be hung.*

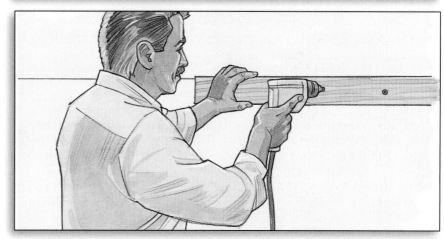

6 *Fasten 1×3 ledgers by driving 2½-inch screws into the studs, aligning the top edge of the ledger on your wall cabinet reference line. The ledger will serve as a temporary support for the upper cabinets and will be removed after installing them.*

HANGING NEW WALL CABINETS

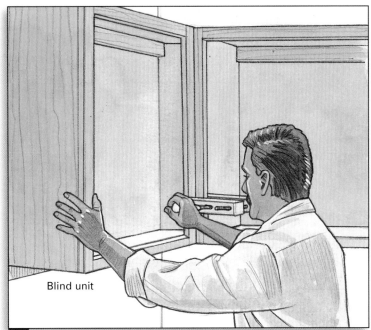

Blind unit

Wall cabinets are installed in two stages. In the first stage, the starting cabinet is hung loosely on the wall. Successive cabinets are in turn installed loosely and their face frames are fastened to each other. In the second stage, the entire run is leveled and plumbed, then tightened to the wall securely.

INSTALLATION TIPS

■ Hang wall cabinets before installing the base units, including vanities. This will allow easy access to the wall work area.

■ Fasten a 1×3 ledger to the wall as shown in the illustrations, making sure you screw it to the studs. The board will give you a temporary ledge upon which to set the cabinets while you're attaching them to the studs. Place the ledger 18 to 20 inches above the base cabinet reference line (19½ inches is shown in these illustrations). Remove the ledger when the units are in place.

■ Cut lengths of 2×4 to fit snugly between the floor and the bottom of the cabinets. Slip these posts under the front edge of the cabinet to hold it while you are driving screws into the studs. Get someone to help whenever possible.

1 Test-fit the blind corner unit with its adjoining cabinet to make sure the doors will clear. You can do this on the floor, keeping the cabinets at right angles to each other with a framing square. Clamp the cabinets together and hoist the clamped unit in place on the ledger. Make any necessary adjustments and mark the blind unit where the next cabinet joins it. Mark the wall for the location of the blind unit, take the cabinets down, and unclamp them.

2 Hoist the blind unit in place and align it with the marks on the walls. Drill pilot holes through the back of the cabinet into the studs, using the stud markings on the ledger. Fasten the cabinet with 2½-inch panhead screws with collar washers, leaving the screws loose by about ¼ inch to allow for final adjustment.

3 Hoist the next cabinet in place, align it with the blind unit, and clamp the face frames together. Fasten the face frames with No.10 flathead wood screws in counterbored holes. Use screws that are long enough to penetrate the second frame by at least half its width. Fasten the cabinet to the walls at the studs.

Insert wood shims at back of cabinet to bring it plumb

4 Position and clamp each unit, fastening the face frames and attaching the cabinet loosely to the wall. When you have installed the entire run, check each unit to make sure it is plumb. Insert wood shims under the back of the cabinets where necessary to plumb them and tighten the cabinets securely. Remove the ledgers.

TOOLBOX

- Tape measure
- 4-foot level
- Cordless drill
- Hand screws (clamps)
- Utility knife
- Screwdriver tips and counterbore bit
- Framing square

FOR MEDICINE CABINET
- Reciprocating saw
- Drywall saw
- Chalk line
- Pry bar

■ Prepare cabinets for vent hoods and plumbing as required before beginning the job. Follow the manufacturer's instructions and use templates if available when cutting holes in the back or base of the unit.

■ Begin installation with a corner or blind unit and work your way across the run.

■ Before fastening face frames, make sure they are exactly flush on top and bottom.

■ Use a filler strip to space a blind unit so adjacent doors open freely. Use a filler strip to fill the gap between the end of a run and the wall. Cut the strip to conform to the space and scribe it if necessary to follow an out-of-plumb or uneven wall.

■ The installation shown here is for framed cabinets. Frameless cabinets install in the same way. Where illustrations show the fastening of face frames, use 1¼-inch flathead wood screws to attach the cabinet sides together.

■ Predrill all screw holes—a split frame can ruin a cabinet and negate your hard work.

INSTALLING MEDICINE CABINETS

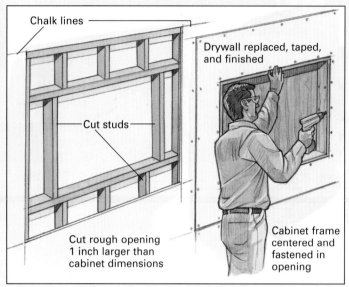

Chalk lines

Drywall replaced, taped, and finished

Cut studs

Cut rough opening 1 inch larger than cabinet dimensions

Cabinet frame centered and fastened in opening

To install a surface-mounted medicine cabinet, use the same techniques as you would for any other hanging cabinet. Make sure you drive the mounting screws into the studs.

TO INSTALL A RECESSED CABINET, FOLLOW THESE STEPS:

■ Mark the outline of the cabinet—level and centered on the faucets—on the wall. Then mark another outline for the rough opening that is 1 inch larger than the original on all sides.

■ Find the studs and mark their centers on the wall.

■ Cut a small hole in the wall with a drywall saw and reach into the recess to check for wiring or other obstructions. Remove any insulation.

■ Cut the rough opening outline and remove the drywall and nails with a pry bar.

■ Cut any studs within the outline with a reciprocating saw, taking care not to cut the opposite wall. Cut nails from the opposite wall with a hacksaw and remove the studs.

■ Measure the distance between the remaining studs and install blocking between the studs at the top and bottom of the opening. Cut the drywall back to these studs if necessary.

■ Install side studs between the blocking at the dimensions of the rough opening.

■ Slide the cabinet in place, centering and leveling it with shims. Attach the cabinet to the studs.

■ Repair and refinish the drywall as necessary.

5 *Cut off shim ends. Tack trim at the back of the cabinets to cover any gaps, unless a backsplash will extend to the bottom of the cabinets and cover them. Fasten the trim with brads. If your plan calls for valances over the sinks, cut the valances to length, clamp them in place, and attach them with screws driven from the interior of the cabinets. Install all doors.*

INSTALLING NEW BASE CABINETS

Base cabinets are installed in the same way as wall cabinets. A few differences apply to cabinets that will contain appliances or large pieces of equipment, such as a television, stereo components, or computer equipment. If you are installing base cabinets only, in a children's playroom, office, or family room, for example, remove any obstructions in your work area and prepare it, following the steps on page 60.

following the steps on page 60.

MAKING ALLOWANCES FOR APPLIANCES

Before you start, double-check the location of the refrigerator, dishwasher, or any free-standing pieces of equipment. Each of these will require its own side clearance, generally about $\frac{3}{8}$ to $\frac{1}{2}$ inch, depending on whether it is a stand-alone unit (such as a refrigerator) or is fastened to the frame with screws driven into flanges (such as a dishwasher or compactor).

If you have not already done so, mark vertical lines on the wall to show the appliance recesses, allowing for the appropriate clearances.

TOOLBOX

- Tape measure
- 4-foot level
- Cordless drill
- Hand screws (clamps)
- Utility knife
- Screwdriver tips
- Counterbore bit
- Hole saws
- Jigsaw
- Brad nailer

PREPARE THE FLOOR

Any hard-surfaced floor—wood, tile, concrete, or resilient material—will provide a suitable base for cabinets. Carpet, however, is too soft to allow you to properly level and plumb the cabinets. If you have carpet on the floor in the location of your cabinets, cut it back and retack it along the base of the units. Check with a carpet dealer or installer if you're not sure how to do this.

KEEP IT ON THE LEVEL

Base cabinet installation requires special attention to leveling. The top of the run must

1 *If the run of your cabinets does not turn a corner, install the end unit first and work your way across the run. Make sure that the total run will not leave a gap of more than 3 or 4 inches at the other end. If necessary, split the difference in the total run so the filler strips are less than 4 inches wide. Shim the unit to plumb.*

Cabinet installed against a corner, no blind unit required

Fill here with filler strip, if necessary

2 *If your cabinets turn a corner, test-fit the blind unit and its adjoining cabinet, then slide the blind unit into place and fasten it to the studs with 2½-inch screws and collar washers. Leave the screws slightly loose to allow for final adjustment. Set the next cabinet in place and clamp the face frames together.*

Blind unit

be level and on the same plane. If the cabinets are not level and flush along the top, the countertop will bend or crack when you tighten the fasteners that attach it to the cabinets. Find the high point on the floor and mark a horizontal reference line on the wall (see page 60). You will set the top of the cabinet run along this line.

GETTING STARTED

Start in a corner, either with a single unit (if the run does not turn the corner), a true corner cabinet, or a blind unit.

■ If using a blind unit, set it and its adjoining cabinet flush against both walls. Insert wood shims along the back of the cabinet base to level it along the horizontal reference line and along the front to plumb it.

■ Next, open and close the doors and drawers on the blind unit, and pull it away from the back wall to allow the doors and drawers to open and close without hitting the other cabinet. Do the same for the adjoining cabinet.

■ When the units are properly placed, secure the blind unit loosely to the wall. Then cut a filler strip to the width of the gap between the cabinets. Test-fit the filler strip and mark its location on the blind unit.

3 *Drill counterbored holes in the face frame stiles and fasten the face frames together with No.10 flathead wood screws. Use a screw long enough to penetrate the adjoining face frame by half its width. Attach the cabinet to the wall with 2½-inch collared screws.*

Ledgers added to support countertop

4 *If your corner unit does not extend all the way to the adjoining wall, install permanent ledgers to support the countertop. Cut 1×3 stock to fit the spaces between the units and fasten them to the studs with 2½-inch screws. Make sure the ledgers are flush with the horizontal reference line.*

5 *Where appliance pipes, plumbing, heating or exhaust vents, or electrical outlets require openings, measure their location carefully on the wall and transfer these locations to the back of the cabinet. Cut small openings with a hole saw, large openings with a jigsaw.*

INSTALLING NEW BASE CABINETS
continued

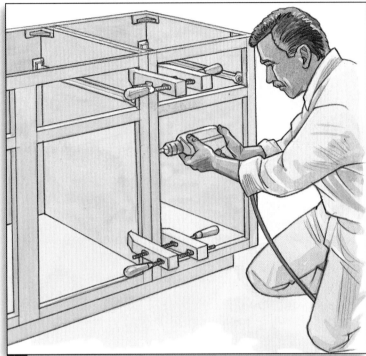

6 Slide each successive cabinet unit into position and install it as you did the first units, clamping and screwing the stiles together and attaching the unit loosely to the wall with collared wood screws.

Toe-kick

Floor   Shim

7 After you have fastened all the cabinets, recheck to make sure each is plumb and level. Insert shims under the rear of the cabinet to bring it level with the line and under the front of the cabinet base to plumb it. Secure the units tightly, cut off the shims, and cover them with quarter round or other trim.

■ Pull out the adjoining cabinet and clamp the filler strip to the side of the frame. Drive screws through the frame into the filler strip. Move the cabinet back into place and attach it loosely to the wall, shimming it for plumb and level as necessary.

■ Leave both cabinets loosely attached for now; do not cut the excess off the shims yet. You can cut the shims after making final adjustments to the entire run.

■ If your blind unit does not extend all the way to the wall, install 1×3 ledgers as shown in illustration 4 on page 65. The ledgers will provide continuous support for the back edge of the countertop.

■ When the units are secured to the wall, secure the filler strip by driving screws from the inside of the blind unit.

CONTINUING THE RUN

Using the same techniques described above, install each succeeding cabinet, shimming to plumb and level, fastening the face frames together, and fastening the units loosely to the wall studs.

If you have a gap between the final cabinet in the run and the wall, measure, scribe, and cut the filler strip before completing installation of this unit.

■ Slide the cabinet into place, flush against the back wall.

■ Shim for plumb and level.

■ Clamp the face frames together but do not screw them.

■ Measure the width of the gap and cut a filler piece to this width, scribing it if necessary to conform to the wall.

■ Unclamp the frames, pull the cabinet out, clamp the filler piece to the end, and screw it to the final unit.

■ Replace the unit, fasten it to the wall, and clamp and fasten the face frames.

FINISHING UP

When all the units are in place, readjust the shims as necessary to bring the entire run level along the reference line and plumb along its length.

Tightening the units securely to the wall may cause some of them to shift slightly. Readjust the shims as you go. Cut off the excess shim stock and cover the exposed shims and gap at the floor with the trim of your choice. Use brads or small finishing nails to fasten wood trim. An air or electric brad nailer is handy for this because it fits under the cabinet base where driving brads with a hammer might be difficult.

INSTALLING A BATHROOM VANITY

To install a single-unit vanity, follow the same steps as you would for any other base cabinet. Place it on the highest point of the floor, shim it both plumb and level, and attach it to the wall studs. To set a multiple-unit cabinet, install the units with their face frames screwed together.

Although standard vanity heights are 30 to 32 inches, you can raise the height by adding risers to the toe-kick or between the countertop and cabinet. These additions should be finished to match the cabinet frame.

Most vanities are open in the back to accommodate plumbing, but if yours is not, measure the placement of fittings carefully and drill or saw holes in the back.

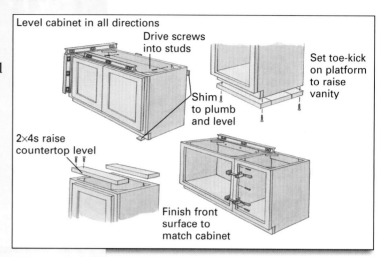

Level cabinet in all directions

Drive screws into studs

Set toe-kick on platform to raise vanity

Shim to plumb and level

2×4s raise countertop level

Finish front surface to match cabinet

FILLING IN

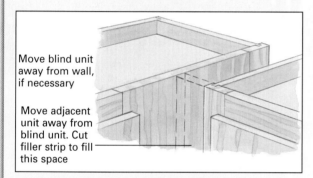

Move blind unit away from wall, if necessary

Move adjacent unit away from blind unit. Cut filler strip to fill this space

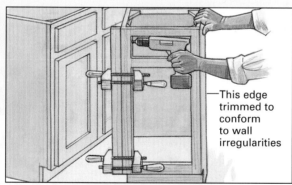

This edge trimmed to conform to wall irregularities

Filler strips close the gaps between blind units and adjacent cabinets and at the end of cabinet runs.
■ Set the blind unit in place against both walls and slide the adjacent unit up against it. Adjust both units so there is room to open the doors and drawers freely.
■ Measure the space between the blind unit and the next cabinet (or between the run and the wall) and cut a filler strip to fit. At the walls, plane or cut the strip to conform to any irregularities in the wall surface.
■ Screw the filler strip to the face frame with No. 10 screws in predrilled holes.

INSTALLING AN ISLAND CABINET

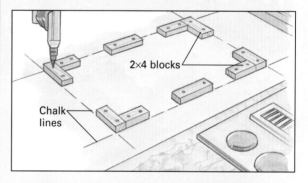

2×4 blocks

Chalk lines

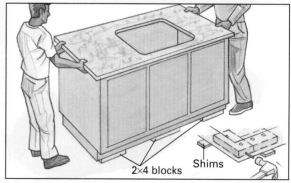

2×4 blocks Shims

Islands are installed over 2×4 blocks screwed to the floor. The base cabinet fastens to the blocks.
■ Set the island in position and mark its outline on the floor with a chalk line. Mark another outline ¾ inch (the thickness of the base) inside the first one.
■ Screw 2×4×10-inch blocks to the floor at 16-inch intervals just at the interior outline.
■ Set the island in place, level it with shims, and fasten the base to the 2×4 blocks with 6d finish nails.
■ Cut off excess shims and install base trim.

MAKING YOUR OWN CABINETS

TOOLBOX

■ Table saw with dado cutter
■ Jointer
■ Doweling jig or horizontal boring tool
■ Jigsaw
■ Router
■ Orbital sander
■ Hand screws (wood clamps)
■ Bar clamps
■ Biscuit joiner
■ 90-degree clamp

With basic woodworking skills and a moderately well-equipped power-tool workshop, you can build your own custom cabinetry. Making cabinets from scratch is a manageable task if you plan, organize, and perform the work in this order:
■ Assemble the case.
■ Build the face frame.
■ Make the doors and drawers.

MAKING PLANS

You can design your own units complete with decorative and functional details, or you can work from published plans available from a variety of commercial sources.

Check the book display rack at your local bookstore or home center. You'll find books on building a variety of cabinets, from bookcases to kitchen designs to units for children's rooms.

The Internet also is a rapidly expanding resource for do-it-yourself project plans. Or you can use the design shown here—a basic face frame kitchen cabinet—and modify it to suit your requirements.

If you choose a design without face frames, you will have to apply wood edging to the exposed edges of the plywood.

Factory-made ready-to-assemble units in stock or custom sizes offer a timesaving option. For these, you provide specifications and plans to the manufacturer, who ships knocked-down cabinets to you, complete with all parts and fasteners.

Whatever source you use, your success will depend on carefully drawn plans and precise on-site layout (see pages 30–35).

CHOOSING THE RIGHT WOOD

Home centers have a variety of materials from which to make your cabinets. You probably

TYPICAL BASE CABINET CONSTRUCTION

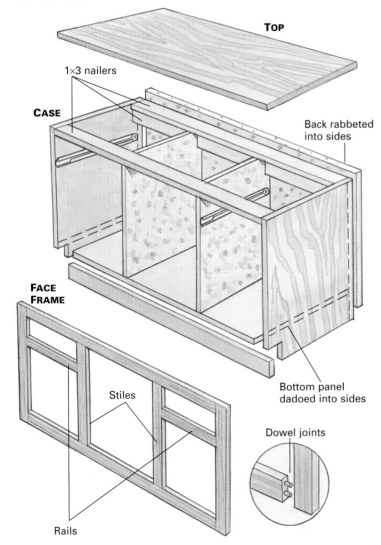

TOP

1×3 nailers

CASE

Back rabbeted into sides

FACE FRAME

Stiles

Bottom panel dadoed into sides

Dowel joints

Rails

AVOIDING MISTAKES

Cabinetry requires patience and precision. Here are a few tips that will help make your project successful:
■ The golden rule of measuring applies at all times—Measure twice, cut once.
■ Schedule your work in increments appropriate to your time and skill level.
■ If you're unsure how to complete a cut, experiment with scrap wood before cutting the real thing.
■ Don't try freehand dowel boring. Use a dowel jig or boring machine.
■ Be sure all attached faces are flush before fastening.
■ Stain first; fill nail holes afterward. This will help match the filler to the stain color.
■ Remove pencil marks with alcohol or solvent; don't sand them out.

CABINET JOINT OPTIONS

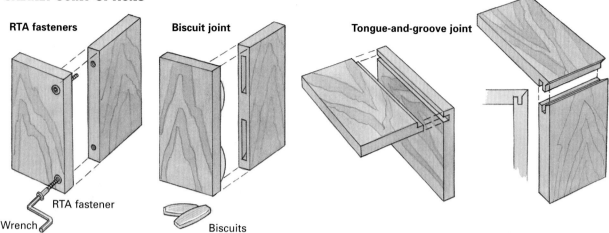

RTA fasteners

Biscuit joint

Tongue-and-groove joint

RTA fastener

Wrench

Biscuits

will make your cases from man-made materials (laminates, plywood, or composites), saving the more expensive solid wood for the face frames, doors, and drawer fronts. Choose the solid wood you want for the doors and drawers first, then pick plywood with a veneer face to match it. Whatever material you choose, buy the highest quality your budget will allow.

■ **MAN-MADE MATERIALS:** This category includes plywood and composite materials, such as medium-density fiberboard (MDF) and particleboard. They are usually sold in large sheets. MDF is a stable material that doesn't warp and has some moisture resistance. Particleboard is available with a thermofused melamine coating, which makes it water-resistant and easy to clean. Cabinet-quality

POWER-TOOL SAFETY

Modern power tools are designed with careful attention to safety, but they still can cause serious injury with careless use.
■ Protect your eyes with industrial quality safety glasses—get the ones with side shields or wear a full face shield.
■ Wear ear protection to avoid hearing loss from long-term exposure to power-tool noise. Find protection that is comfortable. If it doesn't feel right, you probably won't wear it.
■ Wear gloves for rough work, wrist and back supports for lifting heavy material, knee pads for floor work, short sleeves, and slim-fitting clothing. Wear a respirator when using a tool that kicks up a lot of dust.
■ Schedule your work so you don't feel rushed. Keep the work area clean and your tools sharp and in good repair.

OPTIONS FOR DOOR CONSTRUCTION

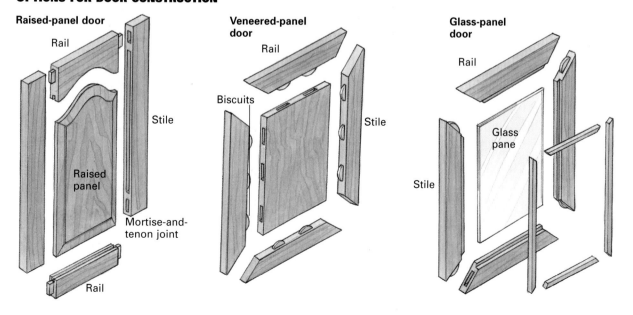

Raised-panel door

Rail

Stile

Raised panel

Mortise-and-tenon joint

Rail

Veneered-panel door

Rail

Biscuits

Stile

Glass-panel door

Rail

Glass pane

Stile

MAKING YOUR OWN CABINETS

continued

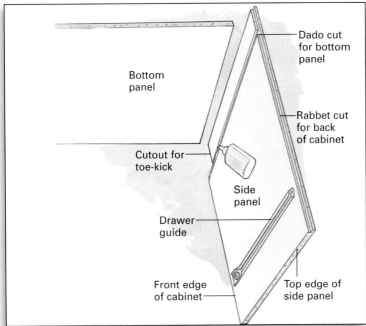

Dado cut
for bottom
panel

Bottom
panel

Rabbet cut
for back
of cabinet

Cutout for
toe-kick

Side
panel

Drawer
guide

Front edge
of cabinet

Top edge of
side panel

1 *Cut the side panels, including the toe-kick cutout. Using a dado cutter or router, dado and rabbet each side where the bottom and back panels will fit. Cut the bottom piece. Install the drawer guides and assemble the bottom to the sides as shown, gluing the dadoed recess and driving 4d finish nails through the side panels.*

plywood, faced with plainsawn veneer in the species of your choice, is preferable to softwood plywoods. Veneer or solid-wood edging will hide the laminations on edges.

■ **SOLID WOOD:** Hardwood and softwood boards are suitable for face frames, doors and drawer fronts. Hardwoods such as oak, maple, cherry, and walnut are popular for stained and clear-finished work, poplar and alder for painted cabinetry. Softwoods such as pine are often used for country-style cabinetry.

ESTIMATING MATERIALS

Your dimensioned plan will help you estimate materials. A scaled sketch will show how to cut the pieces of a cabinet from a 4×8-foot sheet with the least waste. A 4×8-foot sheet is standard, but you may be able to order larger sheets to reduce waste. Consider the size of your workshop and the working capacity of your tools when ordering large stock.

When making a materials list for your face frame, don't forget that the saw kerf (about ⅛ inch) will reduce the yield of the wood. To cut two 4-foot rails, the starting piece will need to be slightly longer than 8 feet. Similarly, you can't rip two 2¾-inch-wide rails from a 1×6, even though the board is 5½ inches wide. That's because, with the kerf, cutting one 2¾-inch-wide piece will leave the other piece less than 2¾ inches wide.

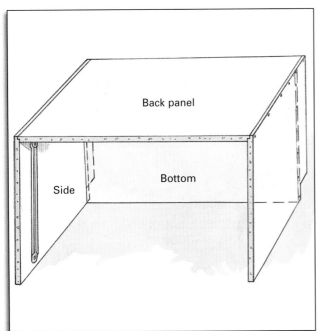

Back panel

Side

Bottom

2 *If necessary, secure the bottom member of the case with a 90-degree clamp, and measure and cut the back panel, fitting it into the rabbet cut into the rear edge of the side panels. Secure the back panel with glue and finish nails as you did when assembling the sides to the bottom panel in Step 1. Clamp the pieces with bar clamps for added strength.*

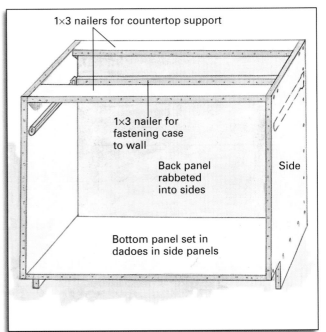

1×3 nailers for countertop support

1×3 nailer for
fastening case
to wall

Back panel
rabbeted
into sides

Side

Bottom panel set in
dadoes in side panels

3 *Set the cabinet case upright on your work surface and cut 1×3 nailers to fit inside the case. Secure the nailers to the sides of the cabinet with No. 8×1½ inch countersunk wood screws in predrilled holes.*

BUILDING THE CABINETS

It's usually best to treat each section of the cabinet as a module, cutting all the pieces to the correct dimensions at one time, then making the cuts for the kind of joints you have chosen (see page 69). Attach internal case hardware, such as drawer slides, and drill holes for movable shelf supports before assembling the case.

MAKING DOORS

Deciding on a door style may be an aesthetic decision, but it will also be affected by the level of your skills. Board-and-batten doors are the least complicated, requiring only the attachment of a batten support to rabbeted door sections. All the other styles shown on page 69 are a variation of frame-and-panel construction. These doors demand more sophisticated machinery and a slightly higher level of skill. Cut all the pieces to exact dimensions and rout the edge of the panel contour. Before assembly, clamp the frame together and rout the panel dado in all sides in one pass. That way the dado will match on all four sides. Unclamp the frame and assemble it with the panel glued in place.

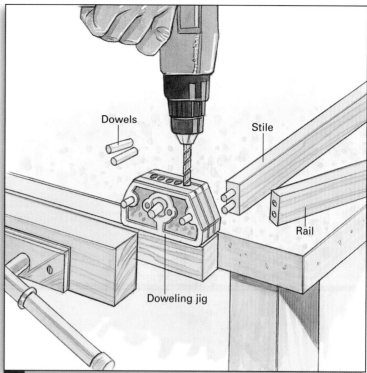

4 Cut all frame members. Using a doweling jig, drill the dowel holes, spacing them about ½ inch from the edge and ½ inch apart. Drill them about ¹⁄₁₆ inch deeper than half the dowel length. Clamp the pieces in a wood vise, apply a thin coat of glue to each dowel, and drive the dowel in with a mallet. With the piece still in the vise, apply glue to the exposed dowels and tap the adjoining piece in place. Assemble in the order shown in Step 5.

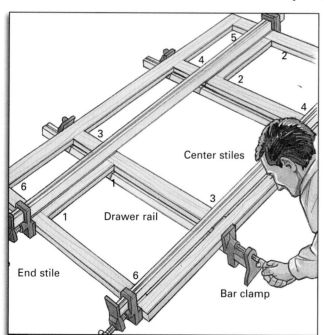

5 Assemble drawer rails to stiles first, and the rest of the frame from the inside to the outside as shown in the numbered sequence. Glue the middle stile to the top and bottom rails, then the two side stiles to the rails. Clamp each section loosely as you go. When you have assembled all frame members, tighten the clamps securely, keeping the frame square.

6 When the joints in the frame are dry, apply a thin coat of glue or narrow bead of construction adhesive to the edges of the cabinet case. Position the frame on the case with all edges flush. Fasten the frame to the face with 6d finish nails. Set the nails. Fill the holes after staining.

You can probably build and attach the base for a laminate countertop one weekend and install the laminate the following weekend. Using dowels to aid in positioning the laminate, as shown on the demonstration surface at right, and trimming the laminate (above) are techniques you will learn in this chapter.

INSTALLING NEW COUNTERTOPS

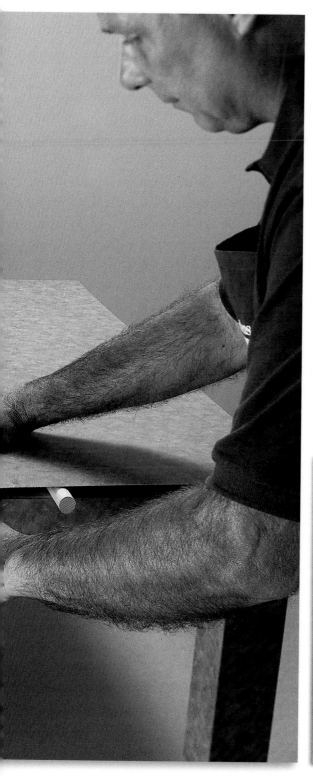

New countertops can completely change the appearance of your kitchen, without any other changes to the room or the cabinets.

This is one alteration that rivals any of the facelifts shown in a previous chapter for low cost and ease of installation. Installing a new countertop will take substantially less time than painting or veneering. You can replace your existing countertop with a post-formed or solid-surface top in less than a weekend. Laminating your own might take a couple of days, and laying ceramic tile, not much more than that.

Countertops make important design statements, so spend some time researching the options before you choose your materials. Even though a countertop's primary function is to provide work space, don't overlook style details such as edge treatments, corner styles, special heights, and backsplash treatments.

SAFETY FIRST

Like the installation of new cabinets, installing countertops is relatively safe, but you should always observe the following safety practices.

■ Wear eye protection and a respirator for any activity that produces dust, and ear protection when using power tools.

■ Always use the right tools for the job.

■ Work patiently and take a break when you get tired. More injuries happen when fatigue sets in.

■ Some countertop materials, especially those made in slabs or complete sections, are heavy and unwieldy. When you lift, bend your knees to keep from straining your back. Enlist a helper whenever possible.

MAKING A NEW COUNTERTOP BASE

A new countertop—except a post-formed or solid-surface product—requires the installation of a new countertop base. Post-formed countertops, manufactured with an integral substrate, and solid-surface materials require cleats and blocks for support and attachment to the cabinets.

Although you may be tempted to set tile on an existing countertop, it's better to take out the old counter and start from scratch. Tile set on an existing countertop may require new plumbing fixtures, and tile adhesion is likely to fail. The increased height of the new materials may be inconvenient to work flow in the kitchen. See pages 38–39 for information about removing the existing countertop.

PREPARING THE BASE

To make a new countertop base, you'll need enough ¾-inch substrate to cover the cabinet frame. Use exterior-grade plywood for a tile or stone countertop—it is more structurally stable and moisture-resistant than interior grades. The smooth surface of high-density fiberboard is ideal for laminate products. In addition, you'll need 1× stock (particleboard, pine, or ¾×3-inch plywood strips) if you intend to install cleats or build-up strips.

TOOLBOX

- Carpenter's level
- Table saw
- Hammer
- Cordless drill
- Jigsaw
- Hole saw
- Framing square
- Try square
- Sanding block
- Orbital sander

Cleats add support for heavy materials such as tile and concrete. Build-up strips are used to increase the thickness of the countertop and are fastened under the edge of the plywood base flush along its perimeter. Cleats go inside the cabinet frame.

Whether you install cleats or build-up strips depends on your choice of surface materials and how you want to finish the countertop edge. One or the other is recommended for particleboard that you will finish with laminate. As an alternative to build-up strips, you can attach a front lip to the base to provide the correct thickness.
- Measure the cabinet dimensions and cut

SOME COUNTERTOP MEASUREMENTS

Although your cabinet and countertop plan may deviate in many ways from the standard, here are a few measurements typical of most installations:
- Depth from front edge to wall: 24 inches, but may be more depending on amount of overhang.
- Thickness: 1½ inches, as either a drop edge or built-up edge.
- Front-edge overhang: ¼ to ½ inch beyond outside surface of doors and drawer fronts. Measure cabinet depth from the wall, add thickness of doors, plus ¼ to ½ inch.
- Side-edge overhang: ½ to 1 inch beyond cabinet frame.
- Backsplash: ¾ inch thick and about 4 inches high.
- Side clearance to appliances: ¹⁄₁₆ to ⅛ inch.
- Island/peninsula overhang: ¼ to ½ inch beyond door surface. If used for eating, 12 to 14 inches. Allow 2 linear feet for every chair.

TYPICAL COUNTERTOP LAYOUT

For laminate covering, center seam on sink to make it less visible

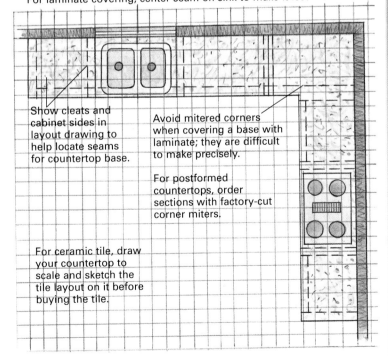

Show cleats and cabinet sides in layout drawing to help locate seams for countertop base.

Avoid mitered corners when covering a base with laminate; they are difficult to make precisely.

For postformed countertops, order sections with factory-cut corner miters.

For ceramic tile, draw your countertop to scale and sketch the tile layout on it before buying the tile.

LEVELING CABINET FRAME

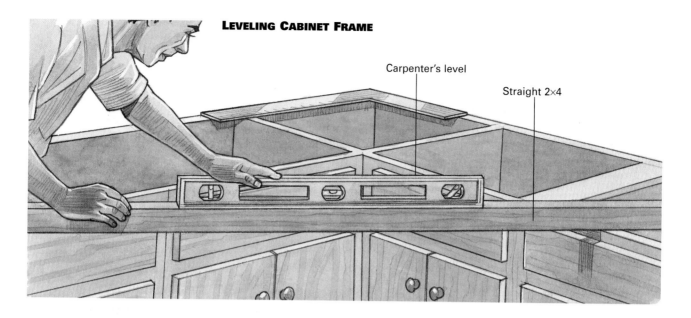

Carpenter's level

Straight 2×4

the base, allowing for the appropriate overhangs (see "Some Countertop Measurements," on the opposite page).

■ Screw cleats to the cabinet frame or build-up strips to the base at the locations shown in the illustration on the opposite page. When fastening cleats or build-up strips, use yellow woodworking glue and No. 8×1¼-inch particleboard screws. These screws will countersink without snapping. Fill the indented screw heads and sand smooth.

■ Set the base in place, contour its rear edge to conform to the wall, and level it as shown in the illustration above. Then screw the base to the edge of the frame or corner blocks.

■ Using a template and following the methods shown on pages 78–79, mark and cut the sink opening. Cutting the opening at this time will allow you to correct mistakes before applying the finish material.

GETTING A GOOD FIT

Countertops must be straight and square along their front edge and level across their entire surface. You must conform the rear edge of the countertop to the contour of the wall and install the base, correcting any out-of-level conditions in the cabinetry.

After cutting the countertop base and before installing any build-up strips, set the base on the cabinet frame with its rear edge on the wall and the overhang centered on all sides. Using a pencil and a wood block that is ¼ inch wider than the largest gap at the wall, scribe a line along the back edge of the countertop. Use a belt sander to conform the edge to the line.

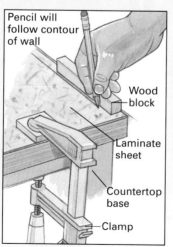

Pencil will follow contour of wall

Wood block

Laminate sheet

Countertop base

Clamp

Shims on cabinet edge level countertop

¾" plywood

Cabinet frame

¾" plywood base   ½" more than front edge of doors

With the contoured base in place, set a 4-foot level on one end of the base and, if necessary, insert shims between it and the cabinet frame to level the base. Continue checking and shimming across the entire surface. Screw the base to the cabinet frame through the shims. Cut the excess shim stock with a utility knife.

INSTALLING LAMINATE ON A COUNTERTOP

Installing laminate on a countertop requires careful planning, but the job is not as difficult as it first may seem. Cutting the material slightly oversize gives you a margin of error that takes some of the stress out of the work.

You can put laminate on an existing laminated countertop or apply it to a new base as shown here (see pages 74–75 for information about building a new base). Laminate will stick securely to an existing laminate countertop as long as it is clean and in good repair.

TOOLBOX

- Metal straightedge
- Laminate scribing tool
- Table saw with laminate cutting guide (optional)
- Router or laminate trimmer with flush-cutting bit
- Brushes for adhesive application
- 3-inch rubber roller
- Venetian blind slats or dowels
- Fine-toothed file
- Cordless drill

PREPARATION STEPS

Bring the laminate into the room at least 48 hours before you work with it. Laminate needs to acclimate itself to the climate in which it will be installed.

Make sure the countertop substrate is completely clean of anything that would cause an imperfect adhesive bond—grease, cooking residues, or dust.

CUTTING LAMINATE

There are several ways to cut laminate sheets. The laminate scribing tool shown below is inexpensive but will produce clean, accurate cuts. You can also use a table saw, but be sure to install a laminate cutting guide to keep the sheets from slipping under the edge of the rip fence. A variety of hand and electric shears are also available, some from rental outlets. Cut all the pieces oversize. Apply the edges first, letting them dry and trimming them as you go. Then apply the top sheet.

ADHESIVES

Contact adhesive for laminate work comes in spray cans or as solvent- or water-base liquids applied with a brush. Brush-applied adhesives are best for countertops. Use natural bristles for solvent-base products. Synthetic bristles are fine for water-base brands. Throw the brushes away after use.

You may find water-base adhesives easier to apply. They change color as they cure, which lets you know when the pieces are ready to install.

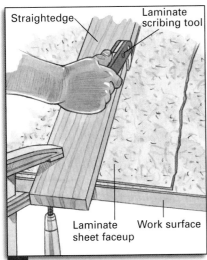

1 Mark the top piece at least an inch larger than the countertop base. Mark the edges ¼ to ½ inch wider than the thickness of the particleboard. Lay the laminate sheet faceup on a clean, smooth work surface and clamp a straightedge along the line. Score the face of the sheet with a laminate scribing tool, making several passes. Keeping the sheet faceup, lift up one side to snap it along the line. Use a laminate guide if cutting with your table saw.

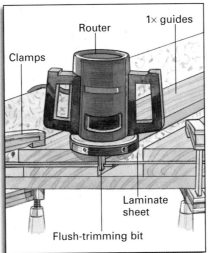

2 Edge cuts on two pieces that butt together must mate precisely. To ensure the accuracy of the joint, clamp two pieces between 1× guides, overlapping them as shown. Make sure the sheets are square with each other and aligned so that the cut line is on the edge of the guides. Trim the pieces with a router equipped with a flush-cutting bit.

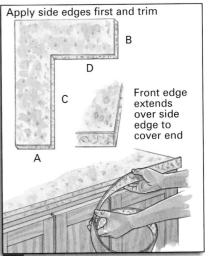

3 Apply the edges before the top sheet. Spray or brush contact adhesive on both the edge of the countertop and the back of the laminate strip. Let the adhesive set up according to the manufacturer's directions. Tack one end of the strip and, coiling it in one hand, work your way down to the other end. Keep an even amount of overhang on top and bottom.

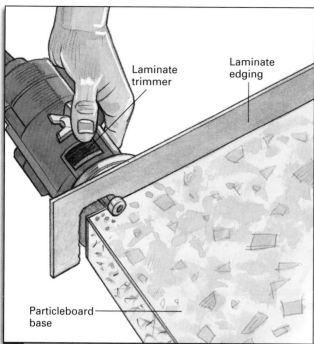

Laminate trimmer

Laminate edging

Particleboard base

4 Use a laminate trimmer or a router with a flush-cutting bit to trim the laminate even with the top and bottom of the particleboard base. To save time you can trim one piece while the adhesive on another edge is setting up, working your way around the countertop until all edges are trimmed.

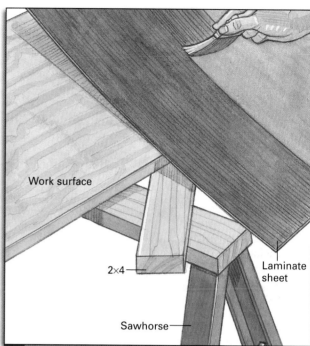

Work surface

2×4

Laminate sheet

Sawhorse

5 With the top sheet cut oversize, lay it upside down on the countertop or other work surface. Brush on contact cement. Make sure that 100 percent of the surface is covered (even if the manufacturer recommends only 80 percent coverage). Remove the sheet from the work surface and set it aside to dry. Apply adhesive to the particleboard base.

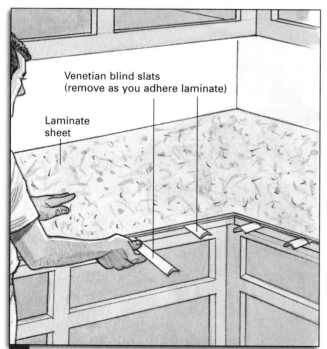

Venetian blind slats (remove as you adhere laminate)

Laminate sheet

6 To keep the sheet from bonding as you position it, lay venetian blind slats or dowels on the base. Set the laminate on the spacers, adjusting it for the proper overhang and aligning it with seam marks. Beginning at the wall or corner, pull out the spacers, pressing down on the laminate as you go. Roll the entire surface with a 3-inch rubber roller and trim the overhangs when dry.

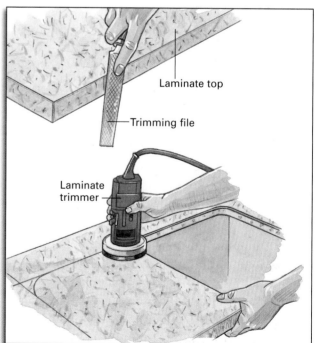

Laminate top

Trimming file

Laminate trimmer

7 Holding a fine file almost flat, file the outside corners of the trimmed edges. File in a forward motion only. Then file the top edges, filing forward and down. Use light pressure. From under the sink opening, drill a starter hole for the laminate trimmer, and working from above, trim the surface to the opening. Install the countertop if you have not already done so.

INSTALLING A POST-FORMED COUNTERTOP

Post-formed laminate countertops (called preformed countertops in some areas) are available ready-made at most home improvement outlets. All you have to do is cut them to the correct length, make some small modifications to conform the backsplash to the wall, and screw them to the corner blocks in your base cabinets.

Manufactured in stock lengths and usually 25 inches deep, most include a rolled front edge to catch liquids as well as an integral seamless backsplash. Make sure that your top is deep enough to overhang the front of the doors by at least ¼ inch. You'll want at least that much to keep spills from running down and damaging the door surfaces. You'll need a separate endcap kit to cover the raw edge when finishing your countertop. Follow the steps on these pages to install a straight section of top. (Miter cuts to turn corners should be professionally cut.)

■ Give yourself plenty of working room so you're less likely to chip the surface. Sawhorses set up in the garage will give you ample space, but removing all the furniture

1 *Measure the length of your base cabinets, adding at least an inch to all exposed edges for the overhang. The counter should overhang the front of the doors by at least ¼ inch. Add only ¹⁄₁₆ to ⅛ inch next to appliance recesses.*

TOOLBOX

- ■ Tape measure
- ■ Adjustable wrench
- ■ Framing square
- ■ Straightedge
- ■ Clamps
- ■ Jigsaw with fine-toothed blade
- ■ Cordless drill
- ■ Belt sander

- ■ File
- ■ Household iron
- ■ Compass
- ■ Caulk gun
- ■ Carpenter's level
- ■ T square

FOR SINK INSTALLATION
- ■ Basin wrench
- ■ Screwdriver

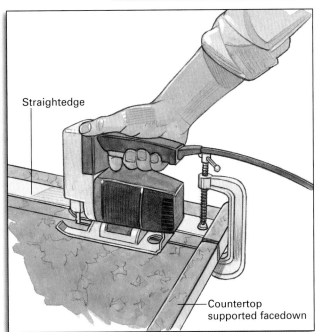

Straightedge

Countertop supported facedown

2 *Lay the countertop facedown on a stable work surface and transfer the cabinet measurements to the bottom surface. Measure twice to make sure your cut will be square. Clamp a straightedge to the countertop and cut with a jigsaw and fine-toothed blade.*

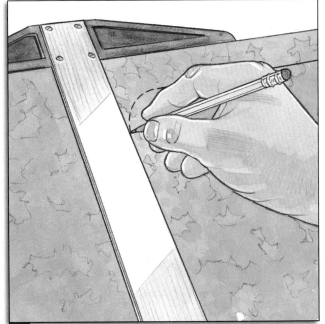

3 *Turn the sink upside down at its location or use the manufacturer's template to mark its outline. Make sure your markings are precise. Use a T square to keep the lines straight.*

from your kitchen and bringing the sawhorses inside will make the job more convenient.

■ Wherever you do the work, support the countertop upside down (to reduce chipping when cutting) and protect the surfaces from scratches with sheets, drop cloths, or cardboard. Cut cardboard large enough to fold around and staple to the sawhorses.

■ Measure the length of the countertop up to any appliance that will abut it. Remove the appliances before marking the scribing strip.

■ Cut the top to length with a fine-toothed jigsaw set for the finest stroke. Then cut out the openings for the sink and appliances. The cutouts will weaken the countertop, so get someone to help and handle it carefully.

■ Be careful when scribing the strip to the contour of the wall. You won't need a fancy compass—a child's compass will do—but make sure the pencil point is sharp and the compass can be securely locked. Position yourself so you can reach as much of the scribing strip as possible in one pass, then move to the other end, if necessary, and complete the line.

■ Scribing a straight or an L-shape counter is relatively easy. If your countertop is bordered by walls on three sides, however, you may find scribing more difficult, especially if the walls are not perfectly square. That's because the

SCRIBE TO FIT

Although the backsplash on your new countertop will be straight and square along its entire length, it's not likely that the wall will be. Most walls have some slight bowing or unevenness, and older plastered walls will often be wavy. That's where the scribing strip comes in. It allows you to contour the back edge of the backsplash to conform to any irregularities in the wall, giving you a tight fit, as shown in illustration 8.

4 Drill a starter hole inside the sink layout lines and insert the jigsaw blade into it. Start the saw and cut the sink outline just on the inside of the marks. Support the cutout from below to keep it from falling and tearing the laminate.

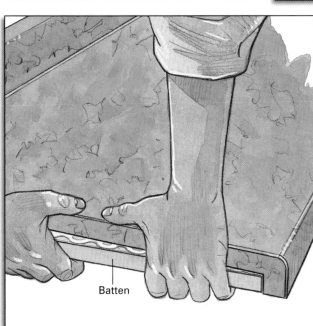

Batten

5 Prepare the exposed end of the countertop by gluing a ¾×¾-inch batten to the bottom. Clamp the batten, making sure it is flush with the end of the countertop. When the glue is dry, remove the clamps and sand the surface smooth with a belt sander.

6 Using the endcap kit supplied by the manufacturer, position the cap with the excess even on all sides. Set a household iron on medium heat and press the endcap on the edge. Remove excess laminate with a file. File only in one direction—toward the countertop.

INSTALLING A POST-FORMED COUNTERTOP
continued

longest dimension of the counter must equal the widest span between the walls, and this length will prevent the countertop from fitting between the narrowest points. This means you won't be able to position the countertop for a proper fit. If you have this situation, you may want to hire a carpenter or cabinet installer. End splashes made of ¾-inch-thick material covered with laminate are often installed when countertops must fit between two walls.

■ If your base cabinets do not have corner blocks, put corner blocks in them before fitting the countertop. Cut triangles from solid wood; glue and screw them to the corners of the frame flush at the top.

7 *Set the countertop in place and level it with shims. Mark the placement of the shims and make sure all the doors and drawers open freely.*

8 *With the countertop against the wall, set a compass at a width equal to the widest gap between the countertop and the wall. Starting at one end and continuing along its entire length, draw the compass point along the wall, marking a line on the top of the scribing strip, the top of the backsplash against the wall.*

SETTING IN THE SINK

There are three kinds of sinks—self-rimming, rimmed, and undermounted—and each requires slightly different installation methods.

■ Self-rimming sinks are held in place by their own weight, the shape of their rims, and caulking. You'll need to turn the sink upside down, apply a bead of caulk around the edges, and—holding it by the drain hole—lower it into the opening.

■ Rimmed sinks are held in place by brackets and a metal rim. To install this type, apply a bead of caulk around the rim on the underside. Set the sink upside down on the rim and fasten the lip of the sink to the rim with tabs or clips. Set the sink in the opening and tighten the clips.

■ Undermounted sinks are hung on the bottom edge of the countertop with clips. Have someone help hold the sink from under the cabinet and tighten the clips.

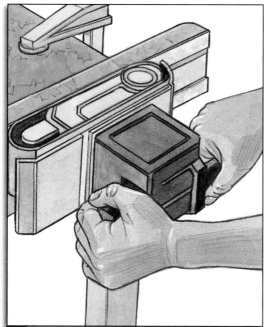

9 Remove the countertop and clamp it to a worktable so you will have access to the rear of the backsplash. Use a belt sander to conform the backsplash to the contour line. Use light pressure—a belt sander takes wood off quickly. Set the countertop back in place. Caulking will cover remaining minor gaps.

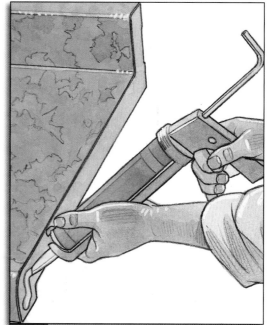

10 Dry-fit seams and make sure the backsplash of both legs conforms to the wall. Apply a bead of silicone caulk to the edges and bring the legs together. Tighten the legs with the take-up bolts from below, making sure that the countertop surfaces are flush.

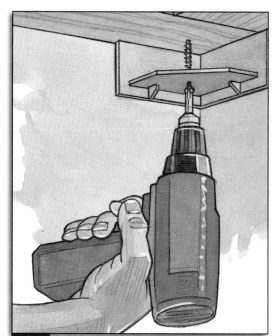

11 Reinsert shims at the locations of your marks and recheck the countertop to make sure it is level. From underneath, attach the countertop to the cabinet by driving screws through the corner blocks. The screws should penetrate the countertop substrate by ½ inch but should not poke through the top.

12 Cut off excess shims with a sharp utility knife and use silicone caulk to fill the seam between the backsplash and the wall. Smooth the caulk with a wet sponge or finger and wipe off the excess.

INSTALLING CERAMIC TILE

Setting tile on a countertop is somewhat more complicated than installing other surfaces, so this project requires additional planning.

DRAWING THINGS OUT

Before you begin the work, make a sketch of your countertop showing approximately how you want the finished pattern to look.

When planning your layout, try to make the tiles an equal width on the borders of the countertop. If possible, make them at least a half-tile wide. Adjusting the width of the grout joint can often make just enough difference that the tiles fit evenly. Take your sketch to a tile outlet to find tiles that will match your layout.

WHAT KIND OF TILES?

Countertop tile must be highly water-resistant and durable enough to withstand dropped utensils and cookware. Most tile suited for countertops is vitreous—dense, hard, and highly water-resistant.

Glazed tiles also are good for countertops. Make sure the tile you choose will not scratch easily—take a sample home and see if you can scratch it with a table knife. If you can, you should consider choosing another tile. If you still want to use that tile, you could install a section of wood countertop or a cutting board in the area where you'll be chopping and slicing.

Before you buy the tile, set several samples on the countertop to test-fit the layout. Space the tiles with plastic spacers equal in thickness to the grout joint you will use. Test-fit the trim also. You can use bullnose tiles with rounded edges, V-cap edging (which is right-angled and fits over the front and top edges), or decorative trim in both bullnose or V-cap. Make sure trim tiles are available to match the tile you choose. Some manufacturers don't make trim for all types. Matching trim from another company could be difficult.

In addition to the tile, purchase grout and caulk with a matching color, and buy all materials from the same distributor so they will be compatible with each other and with your installation.

TOOLBOX

- Measuring tape
- Putty knife
- Cordless drill
- Framing square
- Tile cutter
- Tile nippers
- Notched trowel
- Caulk gun
- Grout float
- Grout sponge
- Straightedge
- Chalk line
- Carbide scriber
- Tile spacers
- Rags

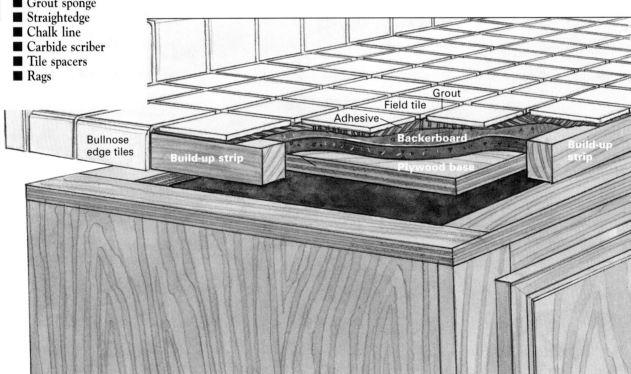

The combined weight of ceramic tile and substrate is heavy and requires a solid, stable surface to keep it from cracking. The foundation for a tiled countertop begins with the installation of frame supports, if necessary, followed by a plywood core and cement backerboard. Tile is then adhered with thinset mortar.

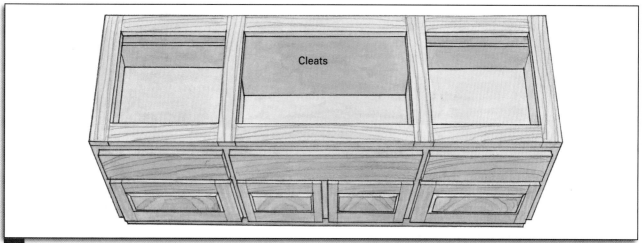

Cleats

1 *Certain installations over long runs may require the addition of support cleats. Screw or finish-nail 1×3 stock to the cabinet frame around its perimeter and* every 24 inches within it. Cut the plywood base ¼ inch longer than the cabinet dimensions. Screw the base to the cabinet, leveling it with shims.

2 *Install 1×2 strips with glue and 6d finishing nails, flush with the top of the plywood base.*

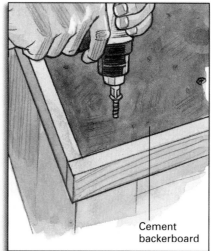

Cement backerboard

3 *Cut backerboard to fit the base. Trowel thinset onto the base and screw down the backerboard.*

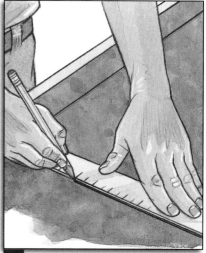

4 *Scribe the sink outline with a straightedge and cut it with a jigsaw and a fine-toothed blade.*

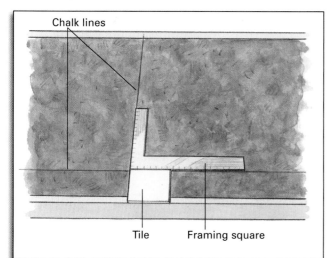

Chalk lines

Tile   Framing square

5 *Snap one chalk line at the midpoint of the surface and another at the point where your edge tile or V-cap edging will fall. Make sure the lines are perpendicular—use a framing square to check them.*

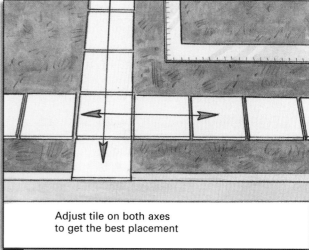

Adjust tile on both axes to get the best placement

6 *Dry-fit tiles on both axes and adjust them until the edge tiles are equal and, if possible, at least a half-tile wide. Use spacers that are the thickness of the grout joints and allow ¼ inch between the tile and the wall.*

INSTALLING CERAMIC TILE
continued

BUILDING THE SUBSTRATE

Tile countertop bases require the same stability as subfloors for tile, and are constructed in much the same fashion, with a plywood base covered with cement backerboard. Cement backerboard is a mortar-base material reinforced with fiberglass mesh. It provides a stable surface for installing tile with thinset mortar adhesive.

Remove the old countertop, following the instructions on pages 38–39. Then install cleats and attach a new base cut from ¾-inch exterior-grade plywood. (See pages 74–75.)

For a kitchen or bath countertop, you should lay a waterproofing membrane over the base because liquids are likely to be spilled on the countertop. Waterproofing is not expensive—either 15-pound felt paper or 6-mil polyethylene sheet works well—and the small additional cost will protect the plywood base against moisture damage in the long run. Staple the membrane to the plywood.

Cut the backerboard so that it fits flush to the countertop edges on all sides. Leave the front and back of the sink opening until last, then cut pieces to fit. Trowel an even coat of thinset mortar on the base or over the membrane and screw the backerboard to the plywood with backerboard screws. Don't use drywall screws; they tend to snap in backerboard.

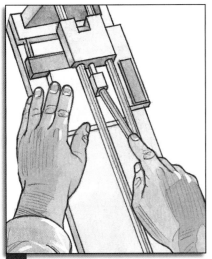

7 Cut straight cuts on a snap cutter or wet saw after marking the tile for the correct width.

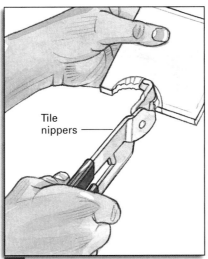

8 Scribe curved cuts with a carbide scriber and nip out the recess with tile nippers.

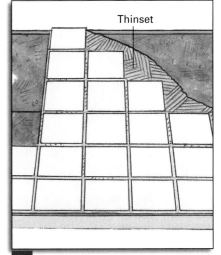

Thinset

9 Working in sections, spread thinset mortar on the backerboard with a notched trowel. Lay the field tiles first, setting them in the mortar with a slight twist. Set tiles in quadrants with their edges exactly on the chalked layout lines. Use spacers and check them frequently with a straightedge as you go.

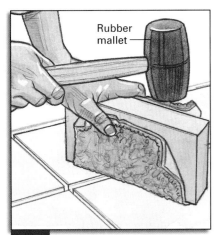

Rubber mallet

10 Level the tiles with a 2×4 block with carpet tacked to it. Gently tap the block with a rubber mallet. Pull up low tiles, apply more thinset to the back, and reset them.

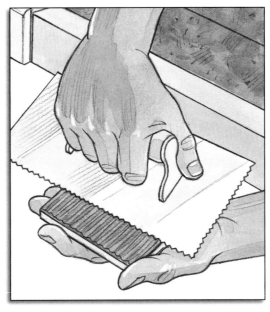

11 When the field tiles are set, lay the edge tiles and the front trim. Backbutter the front trim tiles and make sure their top surface is flush with the surface of the countertop tile.

MARKING THE LAYOUT

Setting the tile will be easier and the result will look more professional if you lay out the surface in grids. Start by chalking reference lines on the backerboard, either at the midpoint of a countertop section or at least 2 feet from an edge. Snap chalk lines at a point where a grout joint will fall in the final installation. Use your layout sketch or dry-lay the tiles to locate the line. For large tile, lay out a distance equal to the size of the tile equally in both directions. For small tile, evenly mark grids that will contain two or three tiles.

SETTING THE TILE

Using a notched trowel, spread and comb a coat of thinset on the backerboard, keeping it just at the edge of your layout grid. Start with the field tiles first, setting each with a slight twist and spacing them with plastic spacers. Check your work often with a straightedge so the tiles will line up.

Work in sections and don't apply more thinset than you can use before it begins to set up. Level the tile with a beater bar—a scrap of 2×4 with carpet wrapped around it— and wipe excess thinset from the surface of the tile. When all the field tiles are laid, let the mortar cure. Wait until the next day to cut and set the tiles around the edge, then let them dry.

Mix grout in a clean container and force it into the joints with a grout float held at a 45-degree angle. Clean off the excess grout with the float held almost perpendicular to the tile. When the grout is almost dry, smooth it with a grout sponge and clean the surface at least twice with a damp, clean sponge. When the grout is cured, scrub off any haze with a soft, clean rag.

TRIMMING THE INSTALLATION

If you are using bullnose or V-cap edging, first trowel thinset on the countertop edge. Then apply more thinset to the back of the trim tiles (a procedure called *backbuttering*).

Set the trim in place, centering it between the grout lines of the top tile. Even if it's not cut exactly to length, you won't notice slight differences. Grout and clean the tile and seal all the grout joints.

To install a wood edge, finish-nail the trim to the countertop surface. Set the nailheads below the surface with a nail set and fill the holes with wood filler after you've stained the trim. That way, you'll get a better color match. Or, you can fasten the trim with screws into counterbored and plugged holes or with hidden biscuit joints.

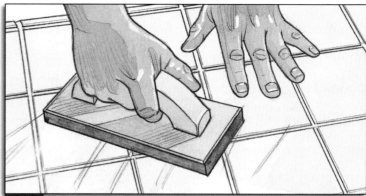

12 Mix grout according to the manufacturer's directions and force it into the grout joints with a grout float held at about 45 degrees. Remove the excess with the float held perpendicular to the surface. When the grout has set slightly, clean the tile with a wrung-out sponge. Wipe the haze with a clean rag.

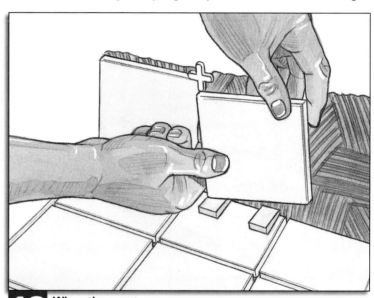

13 When the grout has cured completely, seal it with the sealer recommended by the manufacturer. Dry-lay a few backsplash tiles set on wedges to establish the correct gap between them and the countertop tiles (about ⅛ inch). Then install, grout, and clean the backsplash tiles, following the steps shown previously. Caulk the joint at the bottom of the backsplash tile.

14 If your backsplash extends out from the wall, apply a bead of silicone caulk to the joint between it and the wall. Smooth the caulk with a wet finger or sponge and wipe up the excess.

INSTALLING A SOLID-SURFACE COUNTERTOP

Installing a single-section solid-surface countertop requires fewer steps than other countertop surfaces. If you have moderate skills, you will find that even seamed sections go on relatively easily.

Before you plan a do-it-yourself installation, however, check with several manufacturers. The product you want may not be available for do-it-yourself installation. Or you may be required to attend an installation course sponsored by the manufacturer. In some cases you may not be able to buy the material without the instruction. Installing a top yourself may void the warranty too. This section covers the basic steps. Follow the manufacturer's recommendations if they are different.

Solid-surface material expands at a faster rate than substrate—especially when heated by countertop appliances—and should not be supported by continuous sheet material. Instead, the countertop floats on dabs of silicone caulk applied to cleats, which allows for expansion and sufficient air circulation to dissipate heat buildup.

Examine the factory edges of the material for damage. If you find chips, rough-cut the piece oversize by ½ inch, then trim the factory edge to the length you need. Use a circular saw with a blade made for solid-surface materials, and smooth the cut edge with a flush-cutting router bit.

Solid-surface seam adhesive comes in two forms, fast drying and slow curing. You can work fast-drying products in about an hour—a definite advantage if you are in a hurry to get back into your kitchen. Slow-curing brands are less expensive and will give you plenty of time to set up the countertop pieces without rushing.

TOOLBOX

- Circular saw with solid-surface blade
- Router with flush-cutting bit
- Straightedge
- Vinyl tape or stretch tape
- Spring clamps, hand screws (wood clamps)
- Putty knife
- Silicone sealer
- Random-orbit sander
- Seam adhesive
- Hot-melt glue gun and adhesive sticks

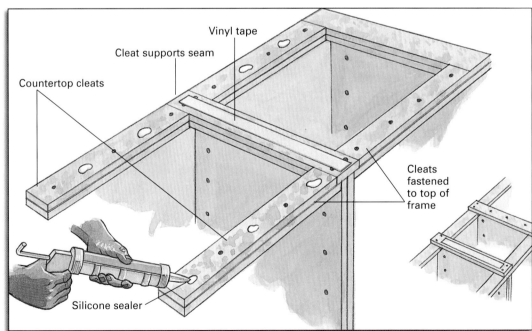

Vinyl tape
Cleat supports seam
Countertop cleats
Cleats fastened to top of frame
Silicone sealer

1 *To support the countertop, fasten 1×4 cleats to the cabinet frame. If your countertop won't have a built-up edge, fasten the cleats flush with the top of the cabinet frame. To accommodate a raised front edge, screw the cleats to the top of the frame. Space the cleats 18 inches on center, under every seam, and on either side of the sink or drop-in openings. Apply vinyl tape to the top of seam supports. If you're installing a one-piece counter, put dabs of silicone caulk at 8-inch intervals on all the cleats and lay the countertop in place, leaving a ⅛-inch gap at the wall. If your installation requires seams, don't apply the caulk yet. Wait until you have all the pieces in place.*

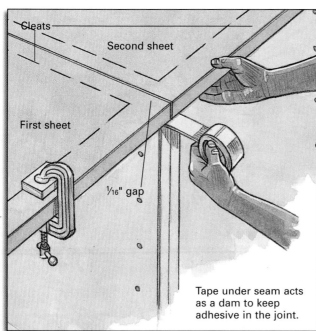

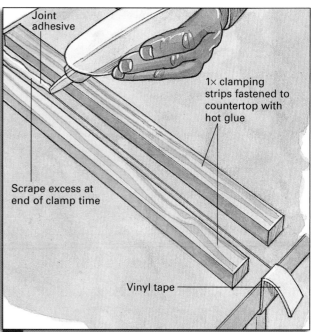

2 Before seaming, dry-fit the two pieces to make sure the edges of the joint will meet crisply. Lift the sheets off the frame and dab silicone caulk on the cleats at 8-inch intervals. Lay the first sheet on the cabinet with a ⅛-inch gap at the wall. Apply adhesive to both sides of the joint and lay the second sheet in place, leaving ¹⁄₁₆ inch between the edges. Tape the overhang as shown.

3 Use low-temperature hot-melt adhesive to attach 1× clamping strips to both sheets about ½ inch on either side of the seam. When the glue has set up, drizzle joint adhesive into the seam, filling it about halfway to the surface. Don't overfill the seam—you'll have too much when you bring the edges together.

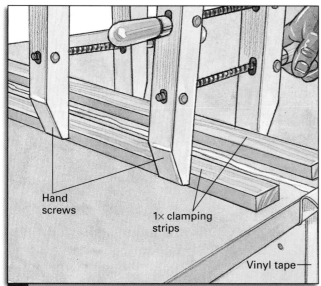

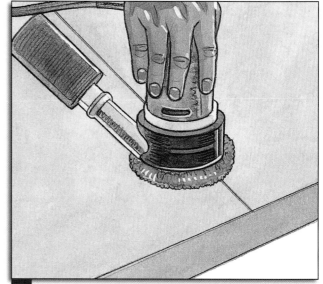

4 Push the pieces together by hand and apply spring clamps or hand screws to the clamping strips. Don't apply too much pressure, or you will force the glue from the joint. After about an hour, or the period specified by the manufacturer, remove the clamps and clamping strips and skim off the excess glue with a putty knife.

5 When the glue is fully cured, sand out any unevenness with a random-orbit sander and 120-grit sandpaper. Use a light touch and run your fingers across the joint to make sure the surfaces meet exactly. Polish the joint further with 180-grit paper and finish the entire surface with 60- or 30-micron polyester film disks or sheets.

Wood cabinets inevitably get scratched, but you can hide the damage with any of several commercial scratch hiders. Start with your regular dust mop spray or lemon furniture polish. Small scratches will often blend right in. If this doesn't work, use a clear liquid scratch remover that soaks into the wood. Other products contain dyes that match the color of the stain. If the scratch is severe, you may have to sand it out and refinish the surface.

You can hide scratches in laminate surfaces that begin to appear with normal use. Several countertop polishes are made especially for this purpose. Get the brand recommended by the distributor you bought the countertop from. Automobile polish can work wonders on laminate surfaces, too, but some kinds contain abrasives that will dull the finish.

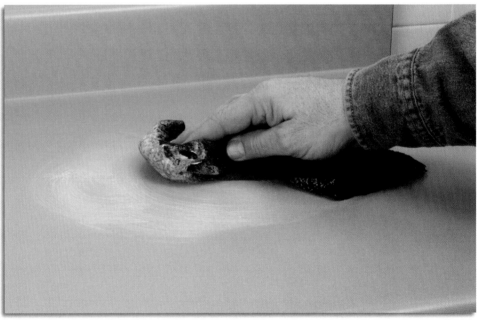

KEEPING CABINETS CLEAN

Kitchen and bath cabinets require regular cleaning more often than any other household surface. Airborne grease from everyday cooking collects on kitchen surfaces, leaving an invisible film that dulls their finish. Hair spray, toothpaste, and soap film collect on bathroom vanities and cabinets. Over time, the collected grease and grime can actually damage the surface. The best remedy is regular cleaning.

Use a mild household detergent and water on painted, metal, laminate, or vinyl surfaces. Sponge off the grime with the detergent solution and wipe the surface dry to prevent streaking.

Commercial household cleaning products that contain alkyl solutions or ammonium chloride are powerful cleaning agents. They will quickly remove fingerprints and grease on painted surfaces, but some will make glossy paint dull. Test these cleaners first in an inconspicuous area; never use these products on aluminum or varnished surfaces.

A number of kitchen and bath cleaners are made specifically for finished wood surfaces. Oil soaps and solvent-based products are safe if used as directed.

If your varnished cabinets become dull with repeated cleanings, furniture wax may spruce them up and provide an additional protective layer. Waxes are also made to add luster to painted, plastic, and metal surfaces.

CARE & MAINTENANCE

Most cabinet and countertop surface materials are tough and durable, and don't require extensive maintenance. From time to time, however, you may need to make repairs or remove stains.

TILE CARE

Ceramic tile requires little upkeep. Regular cleaning with mild detergent will keep tile clean, but never use abrasive cleaners or metal scouring pads. Brighten up dingy grout with household bleach. Remove severely stained or crumbling grout with a grout saw and regrout the tile. Use the same stain-removal techniques outlined for stone (see page 90).

Glazed tile resists almost all stains, but softer tiles, stone surfaces, and grout joints do not. These surfaces need regular sealing. If two years or so have passed since you last applied sealer, it's probably time to do it again. If water soaks into the tile or grout, it's a sure sign that it needs sealing. Clean the surface first and remove any stains, then apply the sealer according to the directions on the container. Seal grout with a sponge applicator; use a roller to seal countertop tiles.

If your tile has severe stains that stain-removal solutions won't clean, you may have to clean the tile with acid. Your tile supplier can tell you whether this method is appropriate for your tile and which product to use. Wear protective clothing, gloves, and safety goggles, and keep the room well ventilated. Scrub the surface with a synthetic pad with a handle, not a brush. A brush will spatter the acid wash on you and anything else in the room.

REPLACING A DAMAGED TILE

Use cutting boards to protect glazed surfaces from scratches, and put insulated pads under hot pans and cooking vessels.

You can replace a damaged tile. Clean the grout out of the joint completely with a grout tool, utility knife, or putty knife. Tap the center of the tile with a sharp cold chisel to break it. Then use a wide cold chisel to pop off the broken pieces. Scrape off the old adhesive and reapply thinset. Apply thinset to the back of the tile and push it into place. Remove the excess mortar from the joint and let it cure. Then regrout the joint and seal it.

You can make solid-surface material look like new with 60-micron polyester film abrasive and a polishing wheel. Add a little water and detergent to speed the polishing.

CARE & MAINTENANCE
continued

Laminate repair pastes come in colors to match your laminate surface. They provide a quick remedy for minor chips. Clean the chip with solvent to remove dust and grease. Then mix the paste to a matching color and apply it with a putty knife. Wash off any haze with solvent.

distributor; chemicals may set the stain.

To make a poultice, mix flour, sawdust, or common cat litter (it's a clay that will not harm your stone) with one of the following chemicals:

For rust—hydrochloric acid and water
For coffee and tea—hydrogen peroxide
For ink and markers—methylene chloride
For oils—ammonia or a degreaser
For paint—mineral spirits

Note that some of these are dangerous chemicals; follow all package instructions for handling and mixing. Mix the materials until they are the consistency of peanut butter and apply them to the stain. Tape a plastic bag over the poultice and let it stay on the stain for at least a day. Remove the plastic and let the poultice remain on the surface until it is dry. Then take up the poultice with a plastic scraper or spatula. If the stain is not gone, but has become lighter, reapply the poultice until it is gone. If the stain still remains, call a stone specialist.

STONE

Stone countertops may require periodic polishing to renew surfaces dulled by scratching and normal kitchen activity. Renewing a granite, marble, or other stone surface requires polishing, honing, or grinding—with considerable skill. This is a job for the pros. Look in the Yellow Pages under "Stone Finishing."

Stone surfaces are porous and must be thoroughly sealed. Even that may not prevent stains getting into the pores. Try to prevent stains by blotting spills immediately. Don't wipe or scrub—you'll just spread the stain. Flush a stained area with cold water, and try cleaning it with a stone soap. Rinse several times. If the stain remains, try using a poultice (see next paragraph). Don't use chemical cleaners without checking first with your

SOLID-SURFACE MATERIAL

Clean solid-surface material with an ammonia-based cleaner and occasionally wipe the surface with a 50-50 mixture of water and household bleach.

Because the color and pattern go clear through solid-surface material, you can remove stains, cuts, and scratches by polishing them out with 60- or 30-micron polyester film abrasive. For more severe damage, use 220-grit sandpaper. Restore the surface finish with the abrasive cleaner and synthetic pad recommended by the manufacturer.

PLASTIC LAMINATE

Plastic laminate resists many stains, such as crayon and most spilled drinks, but some stains may be difficult to remove. Don't use abrasive cleaners; they will leave fine scratches which will make the surface more susceptible to future staining.

Some fruit drink, coffee, or tea stains will come out with a mild detergent and a soft bristle brush.

Dyes used in some beverages stain fast; wipe up the spill at once and pour rubbing alcohol on the area. After a minute or so, apply chlorine bleach, let stand, then rinse with clear water.

For inks, try full-strength pine cleaner or spray alkyl cleaners.

CARING FOR BUTCHER BLOCK

Butcher-block countertops require periodic seasoning to resist stains. Use salad-bowl or butcher-block oil (not linseed or other oils) that is food-safe. Warm the oil first and thoroughly saturate the surface in several applications with a soft cloth or brush. Wait several hours and wipe up the excess with a clean cloth. The seasoning will last longer if you mop up spills immediately and avoid getting too much water on the surface. Clean the butcher block with soapy water. Fill, sand, and oil to repair cracks.

REPAIRING A DAMAGED LAMINATE EDGE

Laminate edges, especially corners, take daily abuse. They can get bumped, clothing can catch on them, and hard or sharp items can chip them. Properly installed, laminate edges can take the abuse, but sometimes the adhesive bond will fail, loosening an edge and making it even more vulnerable.

If the surface is not chipped and is just starting to peel away from the corner, try to reactivate the glue with heat. Set your iron to the cotton blend setting and run it gently over the end of the corner with a towel between it and the laminate. When the glue softens, roll the laminate with a rubber roller. If the end pops loose again, squeeze a little cyanoacrylate adhesive (superglue) into the void and clamp it. Use only a drop—too much glue may bond the clamp to the laminate.

If none of these techniques will adhere the edge or if it is cracked and badly chipped, you'll probably have to take it off. To do that, you will need a thin putty knife, acetone (available at a hardware store), and a small squeeze bottle with a metal tip made for injecting glue into tight spots (also available at a hardware store).

Spread the end of the joint slightly with the putty knife and hold it open, keeping the blade as close to 45 degrees as you can. Drizzle a little acetone on the blade and let it soak down into the adhesive in the gap. You won't need to squeeze the bottle; the acetone will run out on its own.

The acetone works remarkably fast, so as soon as the joint loosens in that area, pry the laminate away from the wood base. Continue working your way down the edge of the countertop, soaking the adhesive and prying up the laminate.

When you're done, remove the sticky adhesive residue with a rag soaked in solvent, and sand the edge smooth, if necessary. Cut a strip of laminate to length (½ inch longer than the countertop if you are replacing a front edge) and ¼ inch wider than the countertop thickness.

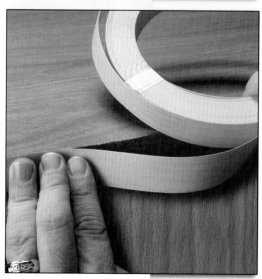

If you're using pressure-sensitive laminate, apply it with an iron, following the manufacturer's instructions. If it isn't pressure sensitive, brush water-base contact adhesive onto the edge and the strip, and let both dry. Coil the strip in one hand, and start pressing it on from one end, keeping the top edge pressed against the slight overhang of the top piece. Continue along the entire surface, uncoiling the strip as you go. Let the adhesive cure, then trim the edge with a laminate trimmer and a flush-cutting bit. File the ends smooth with a fine file and a light touch.

Wood edging is an attractive alternative to a laminated edge, but if you plan to replace the laminate, first remove it completely, as described above. Trim the slight overhang of the top piece with a router or laminate trimmer fitted with a flush-cutting bit. Rip-cut your wood edging to the thickness of the countertop. Miter-cut the ends of the edging, sand it smooth, and prestain it. Fasten the edging to the countertop with 6d countersunk finish nails. Fill and sand the nail holes and apply the finish of your choice.

GLOSSARY

BACKSPLASH: A surface that extends up the wall from the back of a countertop to protect the wall from splashes, often made of the same material as the countertop. See also *End splash*.

BASE SHOE: Small thin strip of wood molding nailed at the juncture of the floor and baseboard molding.

BATTEN: A narrow board fastened across a surface to keep it from warping. Also refers to a board used to provide a straight edge that ceramic tile is laid against.

BEATER BAR: A piece of wood, usually a short length of 2×4, wrapped with carpet and used to level ceramic tile as it is laid.

BISCUIT: A football-shaped wafer of wood that fits into slots to reinforce woodworking joints. Biscuit slots are cut with a biscuit joiner.

BLIND CORNER: Cabinet installed in a corner; storage space in the back is difficult to reach into.

BUMPER: A small piece of felt, rubber, cork, or plastic glued or applied with pressure-sensitive adhesive to the back of a door or drawer front to cushion closing and reduce noise.

BUTT JOINT: The joint made when two flat surfaces meet each other. Butt joints are often glued and strengthened with nails or screws.

CARCASE: The case of a cabinet.

CLEAT: A piece of wood attached to another piece of wood as a reinforcement or to hold another part in position.

CLOSE-GRAINED: Wood species with an inconspicuous grain. Maple and cherry are close-grained species.

COMPOSITE MATERIAL: Man-made construction material usually in sheets, composed of wood chips or fibers bonded under pressure with resins. See also *Medium-density fiberboard, Particleboard*.

CONTACT ADHESIVE: Adhesive that has instant bonding action, applied by brush or sprayed onto both mating surfaces.

COUNTERBORE: A larger hole at the top of a screw hole that accepts a plug to hide the screw head.

COUNTERSINK: To make a hole that is wider at the top than the bottom so a flathead fastener will be flush with the wood; also, the tool for making the hole.

COVE MOLDING: Any molding—usually wood, tile, or vinyl—with a concave face.

CROWN MOLDING: A decorative molding attached at the top of wall cabinets or the juncture of a soffit and the ceiling. Also called a cornice.

DADO: A rectangular, three-sided channel cut across the width of a board. See also *Groove*.

DOVETAIL JOINT: A type of right-angled wood joint that has interlocking triangular wedges and provides superior strength.

DOWEL JIG: A tool used to drill perpendicular holes to receive reinforcing dowels in joinery.

EAR: A small section of any material, such as veneer, left from preliminary cutting that overlaps adjoining surfaces. Ears are generally removed in a subsequent stage of finishing.

END SPLASH: A surface that extends up the wall from the end of a countertop to protect the wall from splashes, often made of the same material as the countertop. See also *Backsplash*.

EUROSTYLE CABINET: A style of frameless cabinet that uses hidden hinges installed in blind holes. Door and drawer pulls are often continuous, integral strips.

EXTENSION STRIP: A narrow strip of wood, usually the thickness of rails and stiles, fastened to these members to allow replacement doors and drawer fronts a wider reveal than the original.

FACE FRAME: Wood stiles and rails attached to the front of cabinet cases to finish the edges, increase stability, and provide a face for mounting door hinges.

FALSE FRONT: A drawer front of the same material and style as doors but without a drawer, usually installed below sinks.

FILLER STRIPS: Narrow pieces of cabinet stock that can be trimmed to fill the width of gaps between cabinets and walls. Filler strips are also installed between a blind unit and an adjoining cabinet to make room for opening doors and drawers.

FLEXIBLE VENEER: Wood veneer with a paper backing. Available in unglued or preglued rolls.

FLUSH: Surfaces that meet to form an unbroken plane.

FRAME-AND-PANEL: Term applied to doors and drawer fronts that have a central panel that is inset and surrounded by a frame. See also *Plank, Raised panel, Slab.*

FRAMELESS CABINET: A cabinet constructed as a box without a face frame.

GROOVE: A rectangular three-sided channel cut along the length of a board. See also *Dado.*

HARDWOOD: Wood from deciduous trees—those that lose their leaves seasonally. Oak and maple are hardwoods.

ISLAND: A cabinet that is not connected to other cabinetry in the room.

LAMINATE: See *Plastic laminate.*

LAZY SUSAN: A corner cabinet with a rotary shelf or shelves built in for easier access to its contents.

MEDIUM-DENSITY FIBERBOARD (MDF): A composite wood sheet material that has fine wood fibers.

MITER JOINT: A joint made by two pieces of material that have been cut at an angle.

MORTISE: A recess cut into the surface of a door or cabinet frame that allows hardware to lie flush with the surface. Also, a rectangular hole in a frame part that receives a tenon to make a mortise-and-tenon joint. See also *Tenon.*

MUNTINS: Narrow wood strips anchored to the interior edges of a door frame; used to divide glass into sections or lights.

OPEN-GRAINED: Wood species that has open pores and a pronounced grain pattern. Oak is an open-grained species.

OVERLAY: The distance on a face frame covered by a door or drawer front. Overlay can vary from partial to full and is determined by door size and hinge type.

PANEL: See *Frame-and-panel.*

PARTICLEBOARD: A composite sheet material made of wood chips, flakes, and shavings bonded under heat and pressure with synthetic bonding agents.

PEEL-AND-STICK: See *Pressure-sensitive adhesive.*

PENINSULA: A cabinet or countertop section that extends into the room on three sides.

PLANK: A door constructed of several pieces of hardwood edge-glued into a single piece. Often has decorative grooves; battens may be attached to the rear to minimize warping.

PLASTIC LAMINATE: A type of sheet surfacing material made of resin-impregnated layers of kraft paper bonded together under heat and pressure.

PLINTH: The base of a cabinet unit, usually separate, upon which the cabinet case rests.

PRESSURE-SENSITIVE ADHESIVE: A thin layer of adhesive that bonds to surfaces on contact; made in various strengths and usually protected by removable paper or foil. Also called peel-and-stick.

RABBET: A rectangular, two-sided groove cut along the edge or end of a board.

RAIL: A horizontal member of a door or cabinet frame.

RAISED PANEL: Term used to describe any of several frame-and-panel doors with panels that have decorative shaping on the edges.

REFACING: Altering a cabinet's appearance by applying wood veneer or plastic laminate; usually requires installation of new doors and drawer fronts.

REVEAL: The amount of cabinet frame surface showing between the edges of adjoining doors and drawer fronts.

RIGID THERMAL FOIL (RTF): Doors constructed of a sheet of PVC vinyl, heat-formed to a substrate of MDF.

SCRIBE: To trace the contour of an adjoining piece or surface onto another piece so it may be cut to fit closely.

SLAB: A flat door made from a wood or plastic veneer applied to a core of composite material.

SOFFIT: An enclosed box installed between the top of wall cabinets and the ceiling.

SOFTWOOD: Wood from coniferous trees—those that have cones, usually evergreens. Pine and fir are softwoods.

SOLID-SURFACE MATERIALS: Countertop material made from polymers cast in thick sheets with uniform color throughout.

SPECIES: A botanical classification that identifies a category of trees and lumber.

STILE: A vertical member of a door or cabinet front.

TENON: An extended, narrowed end on a frame part that fits into a mortise to make a mortise-and-tenon joint. See also *Mortise.*

TILT FRONT: A drawer front that tilts out to expose a triangular metal or plastic receptacle for utensil storage. Often installed in place of a false front on a sink base.

TOE-KICK: The recessed area at the bottom of base cabinets; permits standing close to the cabinets, increasing access to countertop.

VALANCE: A decorative board of solid wood or finished plywood fastened between wall cabinets above a window. Often used to conceal light fixtures.

VENEER: A thin sheet of wood.

INDEX

METRIC CONVERSIONS

U.S. Units to Metric Equivalents			Metric Units to U.S. Equivalents		
To Convert From	Multiply By	To Get	To Convert From	Multiply By	To Get
Inches	25.4	Millimeters	Millimeters	0.0394	Inches
Inches	2.54	Centimeters	Centimeters	0.3937	Inches
Feet	30.48	Centimeters	Centimeters	0.0328	Feet
Feet	0.3048	Meters	Meters	3.2808	Feet
Yards	0.9144	Meters	Meters	1.0936	Yards
Square inches	6.4516	Square centimeters	Square centimeters	0.1550	Square inches
Square feet	0.0929	Square meters	Square meters	10.764	Square feet
Square yards	0.8361	Square meters	Square meters	1.1960	Square yards
Acres	0.4047	Hectares	Hectares	2.4711	Acres
Cubic inches	16.387	Cubic centimeters	Cubic centimeters	0.0610	Cubic inches
Cubic feet	0.0283	Cubic meters	Cubic meters	35.315	Cubic feet
Cubic feet	28.316	Liters	Liters	0.0353	Cubic feet
Cubic yards	0.7646	Cubic meters	Cubic meters	1.308	Cubic yards
Cubic yards	764.55	Liters	Liters	0.0013	Cubic yards

To convert from degrees Fahrenheit (F) to degrees Celsius (C), first subtract 32, then multiply by ⁵⁄₉.

To convert from degrees Celsius to degrees Fahrenheit, multiply by ⁹⁄₅, then add 32.